GRACE
ESSENTIALS

LIVING WITH
THE LIVING GOD

GEORGE SMEATON
& JOHN OWEN

George Smeaton and John Owen have written with characteristic depth on the person and work of the Holy Spirit. Their work, however, can feel somewhat daunting to the contemporary reader and so the treasure remains unearthed. This book resolves that difficulty. A really helpful doorway into the doctrine; it is lucid, accessible and surprisingly thorough for such a short volume. Readers will find it clarifies and edifies in equal measure.

Reuben Hunter
Pastor,
Trinity West Church, London.

GRACE ESSENTIALS

LIVING WITH THE LIVING GOD

GEORGE SMEATON
& JOHN OWEN

CHRISTIAN
HERITAGE

Bible quotations, unless otherwise indicated, are taken from the *New International Version*, © 1973, 1978, 1984, by International Bible Society. Used by permission of Hodder & Stoughton, a member of the Hodder Headlines Group. All rights reserved.

Abridged and rewritten versions of *The Holy Spirit* by George Smeaton (1814-89) together with *Communion with the Holy Spirit* by John Owen (1616-83)

Copyright © Grace Publications Trust 2016

paperback ISBN 978-1-78191-720-6
epub ISBN 978-1-78191-726-8
mobi ISBN 978-1-78191-723-7

First Published in 1998
This revised edition published in 2016
in the
Christian Heritage Imprint
by
Christian Focus Publications Ltd,
Geanies House, Fearn, Ross-shire,
IV20 1TW, Scotland, UK.
www.christianfocus.com

and

Grace Publications Trust
7 Arlington Way
London, EC1R 1XA, England
www.gracepublications.co.uk

Cover design by Pete Barnsley (Creative Hoot)

Printed and bound by
Bell and Bain, Glasgow

Contents

Preface

It must surely be thought a sad thing that there is so much disagreement among Christian believers about the nature of the Holy Spirit and his work. For he is the one divine Person whom we can be familiar with, in intimate personal experience.

He, after all, is the One by whom Christians are born 'from above' (John 3:8): by him believers are taught(John 14:26), by his help believers learn to pray aright (Rom. 8:26), by his presence in them believers keep indwelling sin under control (Rom. 8:13), by his witness believers are confirmed in their faith, and daily guided (Rom. 8:14-16), by his presence believers are to be continually filled (Eph. 5:18), and it is he whom we are not to resist, quench or grieve (Eph. 4:30).

One would therefore have thought that every Christian's experience of the Holy Spirit would be profound, and their knowledge of his work would be comprehensive and unanimous.

Sadly it is not so and has not been so throughout the history of the Christian church. The historical survey in Chapter One of Part One well illustrates this. There has been a succession of misunderstandings and even outright heresies concerning the Spirit, as well as times of renewal both of the experience and the understanding of his work.

That there should be such a variety of views must lead any sincere believer to examine what the Scripture teaches concerning the Spirit. Chapters Two to Nine of Part One seek to do this.

In Part Two of the book, Chapters Ten to Seventeen are concerned with the practical nature of the relationship between the believer and the Spirit in daily experience. The book therefore provides a biblical study both of the doctrine, and of the practice of the presence, of the Holy Spirit.

PART ONE.

The Holy Spirit
(George Smeaton)

1.
Historical survey

The history of the doctrine of the Spirit relates to other Bible doctrines at so many points – sometimes in connection with the Trinity, sometimes with the inspiration of the Bible, the doctrines of grace, the person and mediation of Christ – that were we to attempt a survey of all these debates, there is hardly a point in the whole field of systematic theology or church history which we would not be compelled to consider. But we here, briefly, indicate some of the views of the doctrines which have arisen in the history of the church.

In the very earliest Christian literature – that is, in the apostolic Fathers – we find allusions to the Holy Spirit in connection with the Christian life and experience. The whole doctrine of the Spirit was at that time practical and not merely presented to refute errors in understanding Bible truths.

Justin Martyr (c. 100-165), the early Christian defender of the faith, for example, makes considerable reference to the Spirit in his theological writings, as the 'prophetic Spirit', the 'Holy Spirit', the 'divine Spirit'.

It was not long, however, before the first error concerning the Holy Spirit arose in the Church. This was the error of Montanism (2nd century). The Montanists claimed that they had the supernatural gifts of the apostles restored to them, gifts which had recently passed away with the apostolic age. These men were characterized by disorder, fanaticism and confusion.

Basil (c. 329-379) was amongst those who refuted their error. He wisely saw that the Holy Spirit leads no one to such excesses: 'How can the Spirit of wisdom and knowledge deprive anyone of his senses?'

Another error concerning the Holy Spirit, and indeed the Trinity in general, was Sabellianism (from AD 200). This theory taught that Father, Son and Holy Spirit were only different names for a unipersonal God. The divine person revealed at one time as Spirit was the same person who revealed Himself at other times as Father and Son.[1] Therefore Sabellianism denied that there were any real distinctions between Father, Son, and Holy Spirit.

However, in this system, the Son and the Spirit could have no part in creation, for they had not yet appeared. There could be no atonement for there was no other person of the Trinity to whom it could be offered, and the Holy Spirit's power was nothing but a vague, baseless influence that did not lean on a mediator. Sabellianism was biblically, theologically and practically useless.

Then there was Arianism. Arius (c. 318) destroyed the doctrine of the Trinity by teaching the subordination of the second and third persons (Son and Spirit) to the first (Father). He denied in fact that Christ and the Spirit were

---

[1] Sabellianism: it might be helpful to think of this error in the following way – God is Father, Son and Holy Spirit as the one man may be a father (of his child), son (of his father), and husband (of his wife). In other words, there are no actual personal distinctions, just one person in three different guises or functions.

[Readers interested in a detailed study of church history may be interested in the series of volumes being published by Grace Publications – '*2,000 years of Christ's Power*' by Nick Needham.]

essentially divine; instead they were only creatures. Arius was a rationalist, which means that his ideas were governed by his own reason and not by God's revealed word. He could not understand the doctrine of the Trinity, so he denied it. Needless to say, the Church, in the Nicene Creed (325) and the efforts of Athanasius (c. 296-373), rejected the heresy of Arius outright.

In the fifth century there was a controversy between the Western and Eastern church concerning the procession of the Spirit. The question was, from whom does the Spirit proceed, or go forth? The East answered, 'from the Father only'; the West answered, 'from the Father and the Son'. This controversy is termed the '*filioque*' controversy.[2] The West, following Augustine (c. 354-430), based its views on the words of Christ to His apostles in John 15:26.

Around the beginning of the fifth century, there arose the error of Pelagianism. Pelagius (c. 350-429) maintained that the human will is free and is able by its own natural powers, without the aid of the Holy Spirit, to convert itself to God, to believe the gospel, and to be obedient to the law of God with the whole heart.

It was Augustine who effectively countered this error. He argued powerfully from Scripture that a person's turning to God was all the work of the Holy Spirit. He admitted of course that there was free will in what may be called the 'ordinary things of life', for instance the choice whether 'to labour in the field or not, to eat, to drink, to visit a friend or not'. In these matters, matters which did not pertain 'to God as to love and fear God from the heart', the individual had free will. But where spiritual matters were concerned, he had no free will whatsoever, being spiritually dead.

---

[2] '*filioque*' is Latin for 'and the Son'.

Augustine's biblical arguments demolished the theories of Pelagius. However, a new error soon presented itself. It is known as semi-Pelagianism. It was intended to be an acceptable middle way between Pelagianism and Augustinianism. It asserted that by our own natural powers we are able to take the first step towards conversion, and that taking this step earns us the Spirit's assistance to complete the act of conversion.

It was Augustine again who, before he died, began to counter this new error. He showed the folly of a teaching which ascribed to the sinner the most difficult thing – the initiation of a new spiritual life – and left to God's Spirit the easier task of merely giving assistance afterwards.

The semi-Pelagian error was most fully refuted at the Synod of Orange in the South of France (AD 529). It stated clearly that the whole person in body and soul has been corrupted by sin; and saving faith in Jesus Christ is entirely the gift of the Holy Spirit, not a human achievement at all.

The Reformation

The period of the Reformation (which took place during the late 15th and first half of the 16th century) brought an understanding of the Holy Spirit more full and explicit than had ever been taught since the age of the apostles. Indeed, the Reformation was itself a great work of the Spirit of God, and the men who took a leading part in it were fully aware of this fact.

The Reformers bravely denounced the medieval theology which asserted that sinners could choose salvation for themselves if they pleased, perhaps with some help from God. They also replaced Augustine's tendency to refer abstractly to divine 'grace' with the proper personal ascription, 'the work of the Holy Spirit'.

Following the Reformation, statement of faith followed statement of faith, affirming the biblical doctrine of the Holy Spirit as the One who alone brings spiritual life to souls dead in sin. A couple of examples may be given here:

'Concerning free-will it is wrongly taught that to some extent man has freedom of will to lead a good life; but without the powerful grace of the Holy Spirit, man is not at all able to live a good life and please God, or to fear and honour God in his heart, or to believe in Him, or to cast out of his heart his evil inclinations; these things are the achievements of the Holy Spirit, who comes to us through the word of God.' (*Augsburg Confession*, Article 18, 1530)

'We are so dead, so blind, so perverse, that we cannot see the light when it shines nor respond to the will of God when it is revealed to us, unless the Spirit of the Lord Jesus enlivens that which is dead, removes the darkness from our minds, and bends our stubborn wills to obey the glorious gospel.' (*Scots Confession*, Article 12, 1560)

However, following this period of Reformation and revitalisation, there was a period of spiritual decline. Two errors broke out: Synergism and Arminianism.

Synergism was an error which broke out in the Lutheran Church, and can be traced back to Melancthon (1497-1560, a friend and successor of Luther). It states that the human will has some part to play in conversion, that the human will may and must co-operate with the grace of the Holy Spirit if a person is to be converted.

The error called Arminianism broke out among the Reformed Churches in the Netherlands. Its founder was a Dutchman, Jacobus Arminius (1560-1609). What did he say concerning the Holy Spirit? He maintained that the Spirit's operation in salvation was in every case resistible. The assent of a person's will was what finally decided the matter. Everyone could obey or resist the gospel.

Thus he and his followers denied the free-will of God and affirmed the free-will of man. These Arminian ideas oppose the biblical truth that all the invincible energy of God makes faith the gift of the Spirit of God. They make everything hinge on the human will in conversion, forgetting that sinners have as little spiritual power as merit before God (in both cases, none at all). On the contrary, the natural will and human mind are hostile to God, and the natural heart is spiritually dead as stone.

The Reformed response to Arminianism came from the Synod of Dort in the Netherlands, which assembled in 1618-19. This is as great a confession of faith as any. Its great point was to show that the Spirit produces the whole human response in conversion. Nowhere has the renewing work of the Holy Spirit been more correctly and fully displayed than in the canons of the Synod of Dort. Let us illustrate:

'All who are called by the gospel are seriously called; God seriously promises eternal life to all who come to him and believe on him.' (from Article 8)

'It is not the fault of the gospel, nor of Christ offered in the gospel, nor of God who offers the gospel, that those who are offered the gospel refuse it. The fault lies in themselves, as Christ teaches in the parable of the sower.' (from Article 9)

'But that others who are called by the gospel obey the call and are converted, is not to be ascribed to the exercise of their free-will, but is completely to be ascribed to God, who, having chosen them from eternity in Christ, also gives them faith and repentance …' (from Article 10)

'Faith is therefore to be considered as the gift of God, because God works in the person to produce the will to believe and the act of believing.' (from Article 14)

The Puritans (late 16th and 17th centuries), men like John Owen and Thomas Goodwin, also gave clear and strong teaching on the person and work of the Holy Spirit. They showed that the Holy Spirit is essential in every area of Christian teaching, life and experience. And in this way they freed people from making religion merely a matter of external rituals.

In the middle of the 18th century, the so-called 'Great Awakening' took place in Britain and America. This was a great period of spiritual revival. What happened then cannot be explained in natural terms, only in supernatural. The most prominent names were those of George Whitefield, Jonathan Edwards and John Wesley. This Great Awakening had a powerful impact on the English-speaking world and continued for years afterwards.

However, in the modern period, the 19th and 20th centuries, there have been many views detracting from the divine dignity and personality of the Holy Spirit, particularly those of Schleiermacher (1768-1834) and his followers. This theology reduces the Holy Spirit to nothing more than the common spirit of the Christian Church. It turns out to be a modern form of Sabellianism, where the Spirit is a mere influence.

Allied to this, critical views of Scripture have arisen which reject the inspiration of the Holy Spirit; ritualism, which springs from a desire to substitute the material for the spiritual (the glorious Holy Spirit); and attempts at Christian evangelism which depend not on the Holy Spirit but upon human methods of persuasion. We need always to be reminded that Scripture says, 'Not by might, nor by power, but by my Spirit, says the LORD Almighty' (Zech. 4:6).

This historical survey, which has brought to our attention great periods of revival such as the age of Augustine, the Reformation, and the Great Awakening of the 18th century, naturally suggests a closing remark which is not out of place. The Church of God is in her right attitude only when she is waiting for a fresh outpouring of the Holy Spirit, who comes from Christ and leads to Christ.

2.
Biblical survey

From the books of Moses and Job

Following are a few references to the Spirit in the earliest books of the Bible.

'The Spirit of God hovered over the waters' (Gen. 1:2). The term 'Spirit' (Hebrew '*ruach*') denotes a breath, a wind, and also an intelligent thinking being.

'By his breath (or Spirit) the skies became fair' (Job 26:13). This is a declaration that the personal Spirit – elsewhere called the finger of God and the power of God – decorated the heavens, and framed them to display the divine glory.

'The Spirit of God has made me; the breath of the Almighty gives me life' (Job 33:4). The reference to a personal agent uniquely related to God, from God, but personally distinct, is too clear to be ignored.

Now consider, in a little detail, the words of Genesis 2:7, 'The LORD God formed man from the dust of the ground and breathed into his nostrils the breath of life, and the man became a living being'.

When God breathed into man the breath of life, we must understand by this the life of the Holy Spirit, spiritual life, as well as physical and intellectual life. It does not refer simply to the animation of the body. Before their fall into sin, Adam and Eve possessed the Holy Spirit, spiritual life, but when they fell into sin, the Holy Spirit departed from them, and they immediately died a spiritual death, as God had said.

According to Genesis 6:3 'My Spirit will not contend with man for ever, for he is mortal': the meaning here is that men and women, before the flood, had rejected the message of the Spirit, given by Spirit-filled men, calling them to repentance and faith.

Abraham was called a prophet and therefore had the Spirit (Gen. 20:7). In Joseph we see the same gift continued, as the words of Pharaoh clearly indicate: 'Can we find anyone like this man, one in whom is the spirit of God?' (Gen. 41:38).

As far as Moses is concerned, we find explicit statements that he was raised up and qualified by the Spirit for his great task of leading God's people (Num. 11:17, 25).

The Spirit of God also inspired Moses to commit to writing the word of God, so that it became the great means for promoting the spiritual good of men and women. We see the activity of the Spirit also in that spiritual illumination of multitudes of true believers who love God's word.

Finally, we find later in the Old Testament two noteworthy passages referring to the comforting power of the Spirit during the time of the Israelites travelling in the desert. These words applied then, as now, for all and not merely for a few specially gifted believers: 'You gave your good Spirit to instruct them' (Neh. 9:20); and 'Where is he who set his Holy Spirit among them?' (Isa. 63:11), and 'Like cattle that go down to the plain, they were given rest by the Spirit of the LORD' (v. 14).

From the time of Joshua to David

The Spirit of God is not mentioned in the whole book of Joshua. However, it is clear that the Spirit has not withdrawn, for Joshua himself was full of the spirit of wisdom (Deut. 34:9).

In the book of Judges – a period of spiritual decline – we find repeated references to the Spirit of God coming upon men that they might deliver Israel from their oppressors. These heroes of Israel – Othniel, Gideon, Jephthah, Samson – all owed their extraordinary powers and gifts to the Spirit of God.

Following the chaotic times of the Judges, a period of revival appears in the days of Samuel, the last of the judges. The spirit of prophecy filled Samuel in a special way, and from his time onwards a line of prophets arose. All of these prophets, given to guide the history of Israel, relied upon the Spirit of God to equip them to fulfil their function as prophets. They spoke as prophets of God only as they were 'carried along' by the Spirit (2 Pet. 1:21) and not in their own power.

The result of our investigation up to this point demonstrates that the divine Spirit is no mere quality of the human spirit. Rather, in the very oldest books of the Bible, and in the whole course of history following, He is always introduced as the personal creative Spirit of God.

From the rise of David to the exile

Many of the Psalms were written during this period, together with the writings of Solomon, Hosea, Joel, Micah, and Isaiah. In all of these we find clear references to the Holy Spirit.

When David was anointed by Samuel to be king, we read, 'from that day on the Spirit of the LORD came upon David in power' (1 Sam. 16:13). It was the Spirit who equipped David with the gifts necessary for kingship, and gave him the spiritual quality to remain faithful to the word of God. In addition to this, inspiration was given to him: 'The Spirit of the LORD spoke through me; his word was on my tongue' (2 Sam. 23:2). David though the Spirit gave prophecies concerning the birth, sufferings, death, resurrection, and glory of Christ, David's greater Son.

In Psalm 51:11 David prays: 'Do not cast me from your presence or take your Holy Spirit from me.' David had sinned very seriously against God, and in this psalm, which contains the expression of his repentance, he pleads that the Holy Spirit may not be taken from him. Here, for the first time, we have the word 'holy' connected with the Spirit of God. He is not only the Spirit of wisdom and the Spirit of power, but the Holy Spirit. And in another psalm he is called the 'good' Spirit (Ps. 143:10).

Indeed, the beauty of the writings themselves show the presence of the Spirit in the psalm writers. The power and presence of the Spirit in ample measure must have been conferred upon the psalm writers to produce these psalms.

We come now to the prophets, where we find many allusions to the Spirit of God. We may classify these in the following way: (1) some refer to their own time, and to the way in which the Spirit helped the prophets to fulfil their office; (2) some refer to the great outpouring of the Spirit upon the Church still to come in the future; (3) others refer to the outpouring of the Spirit on the awaited Messiah, the great central thought of Jewish religion, as it is of all revealed religion.

Hosea, perhaps the oldest writing prophet, speaks of 'the man of the Spirit' (9:7 RSV). The prophets themselves were such men of the Spirit.

Joel gives the prediction concerning the great outpouring of the Spirit which is reserved for the last days: 'And afterwards, I will pour out my Spirit on all people' (2:28).

Isaiah and Micah refer, in various passages, very emphatically to the Spirit of God.

Isaiah has scattered throughout his prophecies many allusions to the Spirit of God. In particular he refers to the Spirit as the anointer of the Messiah. He introduces the 'Servant of the LORD' (the Messiah) with these words: 'and now the Sovereign LORD has sent me, with his Spirit' (48:16). There are other similar passages to look up, e.g. 11:2, 42:1, 61:1.

Another set of passages in Isaiah refer to the gift of the Spirit to the Church. For example: 'For I will pour water on the thirsty land, and streams on the dry ground; I will pour out my Spirit on your offspring, and my blessing on your descendants' (44:3). See also 59:21.

From the beginning of the exile to the end of the Old Testament

In Ezekiel, Daniel, Haggai, Zechariah, Chronicles, Nehemiah, again we encounter many allusions to the Spirit of God.

There are no explicit references in Jeremiah and Daniel. Nevertheless, the allusions are plain. Jeremiah was a man described as sanctified from the womb, and, as a prophet, he received some of the most definite revelations ever communicated, particularly the revelation of the new covenant, with all its spiritual blessings (Jer. 31:31).

It is the same with Daniel. We cannot fail to perceive the Spirit's agency in all his interpretations of dreams, in all his visions of the future, and in all his allusions to the anointing of the 'most holy' (Dan. 9:24).

In the writings of Ezekiel, the expression 'the Spirit', 'the Spirit of God', or 'my Spirit', occurs very frequently. See for example 2:2; 3:14, 24; 8:3; 11:24. What is more, all the great promises announced by Ezekiel have very clear reference to the converting and transforming grace of the Spirit promised to Israel in connection with their restoration (36:25-27).

Haggai announced to the people of Israel that, although the external glory of the second temple would be a disappointment compared with the first, they were not to be discouraged because the Spirit of God was among them as a source of grace, light, strength and holiness.

In Zechariah we find two explicit allusions to the Spirit's agency – one for the time of the prophet, another for the distant future of God's people. Amid discouragements which might otherwise have depressed Zerubbabel the ruler, the prophet was commissioned to show: first, that the maintenance of the Church was not dependent on the resources of worldly kingdoms, but on God's Spirit (4:6); and secondly, that the Spirit would be the Spirit of grace to the house of David in later days and bring into effect the national conversion of the people in the midst of the deepest expressions of sorrow and mourning (12:10).

The Gospels and Acts

There was a long pause of nearly four hundred years between the last of the Old Testament prophets and the time when the Spirit of God again spoke by revelation. We no sooner take up the Gospel writers' narrative of the incarnation of Jesus Christ than we find the same important place occupied by the Holy Spirit

All the Gospel writers refer to the Holy Spirit in connection with the birth, baptism and temptation of the Lord Jesus (see chapter 5).

As far as Jesus' teaching is concerned, there is considerable material on the Holy Spirit, particularly in the Gospel of John. For example, Christ promised the Holy Spirit to His believing disciples to quench their spiritual thirst like 'streams of living water' (John 7:37-39).

The outpouring of the Spirit at Pentecost

A new revelation from God to man, as Pentecost clearly was, had, of necessity, to be inaugurated with supernatural signs and miracles. As the setting up of the old covenant at Sinai was accompanied by miraculous signs, so must the new covenant at Pentecost.

The greatest event in all history, next to the incarnation of Jesus and His atonement, was the outpouring of the Holy Spirit, for it will continue, as long as the world lasts, to spread amongst human beings the stream of divine life. Pentecost was the great day of the Holy Spirit, the opening of the river of the water of life, the birthday of the Christian Church.

On that day, the power of the Spirit transformed the apostles: the timid became bold, the selfish became self-denying, and the arrogant became humble.

The Spirit also transformed the understanding of the apostles: they received a knowledge such as they had never had before of the great work which Jesus had fulfilled for man's salvation, and no longer were deluded into thinking that the kingdom of the Messiah was to be of a worldly nature.

But special reference must here be made to those supernatural gifts conferred by the sovereign Christ on the day of Pentecost. These continued all through the apostolic age and were wholly distinct from the ordinary saving and serving gifts which continue in the Church throughout all her history. These supernatural or extraordinary gifts were temporary, and intended to disappear when the Church was established and the canon of Scripture completed and closed, for they were an outward sign of an inward inspiration of the apostles by the Holy Spirit.

These temporary supernatural gifts were: prophecy, tongues, interpretation of tongues, the message of wisdom, the message of knowledge, the gift of faith (not saving faith but miraculous faith), healing and miracles, distinguishing between spirits.

The gift of tongues was the power of speaking in foreign languages which had never been learnt. Peter, unaided, could only speak his Galilean dialect, which easily betrayed him, as we see in the courtyard (Matt. 26:73). However, now, on the day of Pentecost, he could, in company with his colleagues, command without difficulty the attention of educated hearers, who heard them speak in their own language the wonderful acts of God.

Many, interpreting Acts 2 in the light of 1 Corinthians 12, view the gift of tongues as an ecstatic, unintelligible kind of language. But this is a misinterpretation of all the passages concerned. The gift was completely miraculous. The apostles received extraordinary power to utter words wholly unknown to them before, and in this way to express spiritual truth which arrested, convinced and enlightened the minds of those whom the Holy Spirit was leading to the Saviour.

Whatever difficulties we may have in this age with this miraculous occurrence, there can be no doubt that, in the midst of an influx of people from foreign countries, no more appropriate or powerful means could be employed to extend the gospel than that use of foreign languages which took place at Pentecost. This event clearly indicated that the gospel, unlike the limitations of Judaism, was not for one people only (the Jews), but for all people everywhere. It filled the hearers with amazement. To speak a new language by the sudden influence of the Spirit, exceeded all natural powers, and gave a sure sign of the presence and all-powerfulness of the Holy Spirit. But in the church it had comparatively little value, for tongues were a sign not for believers, but for unbelievers

(1 Cor. 14:22).When, therefore, he heard that this gift was being desired merely for the purpose of show, the apostle Paul took the opportunity to rebuke the Corinthians for that perversion (1 Cor. 12:20-31).

The apostolic letters

We are concerned here with the teaching of Paul, Peter, James, Jude and John.

We may very briefly summarise their teaching in the following way. Each takes for granted the general corruption of man's nature, and refers to the Spirit as the author and source of all the saving, sanctifying and strengthening grace which Christians experience (Eph. 3:16; Rom. 15:13).

Paul's teaching on the Holy Spirit is fuller than anywhere else in the New Testament. We can only give a few examples: the Spirit washes, sanctifies, justifies (1 Cor. 6:11); He enlightens with spiritual knowledge (1 Cor. 2:14); He provides the gift of saving faith (2 Cor. 4:13); He is a deposit, guaranteeing what is to come for the Christian (2 Cor. 1:22); He produces spiritual fruit in the Christian's life (Gal. 5:22, 23). We could go on. It is, however, in the eighth chapter of Romans that the teaching on the Holy Spirit is most fully developed, where the apostle's purpose is to prove the certainty of the believer's salvation from the fact that he is led by the Spirit of God.

James only mentions the Spirit once. However, his entire letter takes for granted the necessity of the Spirit's renewing grace. He encourages those who lack wisdom to ask God for it in believing prayer (1:5). He implies the Spirit's agency when he says that every good and perfect gift comes from above (1:17). He assumes the Spirit's work of regeneration through the word of truth as the foundation of it all. The tenor of the letter implies that the Holy Spirit, the giver of faith, first enters the Christian heart as His home, then makes it a temple worthy of Himself.

Peter teaches that the persecuted Christian enjoys the presence of the 'Spirit of glory' resting on him. He also teaches (1 Pet. 1:2) that the Spirit is responsible for the Christian's sanctification (growth in holiness).

In his second letter Peter says that the prophets spoke the word of God only as they were 'carried along' by the Holy Spirit (2 Pet. 1:21).

Jude encourages us to 'pray in the Holy Spirit' (v. 20). He implies a life in fellowship with the Holy Spirit, a life of prayer resulting from that fellowship. Indeed, all true prayer is prayer in the Holy Spirit, who opens our eyes so that we discover our spiritual poverty and the value of spiritual things.

The apostle John speaks of the Spirit in connection with Christian assurance: 'This is how we know that he lives in us: We know it by the Spirit he gave us' (1 John 3:24. cf. 4:13). Just as Paul calls the Spirit the 'guarantee' (2 Cor. 1:22), so John declares that the Holy Spirit given to Christians gives them a knowledge and an assurance of God's love.

And, finally, in the book of Revelation, we find many references to the Holy Spirit. The apostle John says at the beginning: 'On the Lord's Day I was in the Spirit' (1:10). When Christ sends letters to the seven churches, He commands them to hear what the Spirit says to the churches (2:7); because it is the personal Holy Spirit who speaks in and by the gospel. And the book closes with the call: 'The Spirit and the bride say, "Come!"' (22:17) – that is, the Church moved by the Spirit says to the Lord Jesus Christ, 'Come.'

3.
The Trinity

As we consider the doctrine of the Holy Spirit, so we shall necessarily come into contact at every point with the doctrine of the Trinity. It is therefore appropriate to refer briefly to this great doctrine before approaching the doctrine of the Holy Spirit directly.

Though every attempt to understand or to unfold the mystery of the Trinity has failed, and must fail according to the very nature of the subject, we may affirm that the following five statements satisfactorily express the belief of the Christian Church:

1. There is one God or divine being.[3]

2. This one being is common to three divine Persons, who are designated Father, Son and Holy Spirit.

3. There is between these three Persons a natural order, so that the first Person has life in Himself (John 5:26); and the second and third Persons eternally exist and act from the first.

---

[3] 'being': simply refers to what something or someone is; in this case, 'divine being' means what it is to be 'God'; we might say, one who has 'divinity' or 'God-ness'.

4. This order of the divine Persons belongs to the divine being and not merely to the divine operations (i.e. to what God is and not merely what God does).

5. This natural order is the basis and reason for the names Father, Son and Spirit; for the Son is eternally begotten[4] of the Father, and the Spirit proceeds eternally from both the Father and the Son.

Those five points describe the divine being.

As far as the divine works are concerned, we should understand them in the following way: the Father is the *source from which* they begin; the Son is the *medium through which* they take place; and the Holy Spirit is the *executive by which* they are carried into effect.

From the beginning, the Christian Church has firmly believed in the doctrine of the Trinity. The Church found in the baptismal formula (Matt. 28:19) a clear allusion to Father, Son and Holy Spirit, and simply accepted it as a statement of the doctrine of the Trinity. The doctrine was not reserved for scholars alone, but was given in simple fashion to every Christian believer.

The doctrine of the Trinity is not so much one doctrine among many, but it is essential to an understanding of Christianity itself. It not only presents to the mind a high and great subject for contemplation, but it brings peace to the heart and conscience.

It is not our place to explain the Trinity, but to love, treasure and guard the mystery. As one philosopher has said, if we could explain it in human terms, it would be a mystery no

---

[4] 'begotten': this is an old English word and means, 'to be fathered by'; (clearly) the Son is fathered by the 'Father', though obviously not in the same way that human babies are fathered by human parents.

longer. Let every Christian feel the force of these beautiful words from Gregory of Nazianzus (c. 330-390) on the Trinity:

> 'I cannot think of the *one* (God) but I am immediately surrounded with the splendour of the *three* (persons); nor can I clearly discover the *three*, but I am suddenly carried back to the *one*.'

And when we look at the doctrine from the practical point of view, belief of this great truth is absolutely essential to the Christian individual and to the Church. Without it, Christianity would at once collapse. We find that every Christian teaching leads to it, and every privilege and duty hangs upon it. The doctrine of the Trinity is the most fundamental, vital and practical of doctrines. It is the foundation of every truth. It is completely intertwined with the Christian gospel and all it provides, and without it, the whole plan of salvation falls to the ground.

Having briefly considered the doctrine of the Trinity, we are now in a position to proceed particularly to the doctrine of the third Person of the Trinity, the Holy Spirit.

4.
The personality, procession and deity of the Holy Spirit

The personality of the Holy Spirit

We begin by discussing the personality of the Spirit. We must not become so absorbed with the work of the Spirit that we forget Himself, His personality. The Spirit is no mere power, force or influence, as some claim. My aim is to show that the Spirit of God is as truly a person as the Father or the Son.

We have only to recall the language used to refer to the Spirit as 'comforter' or 'counsellor' to be convinced of His personality. To compensate for the loss of the Lord Jesus when He departed to the Father, He promised His disciples that He would send another counsellor or comforter, who would take His place as their immediate teacher, helper and protector, and therefore supply the need for Christ's own presence. Now it is very clear that this 'other', who was to fill Christ's place as it were, would Himself be personal. This is also clear from the fact that the Spirit would teach them (John 14:26); guide them into all truth (16:13); remind them (14:26); bring glory to Christ by taking from what was Christ's and making it known to His disciples (16:14).

The meaning of many Bible passages is lost unless we think of the Holy Spirit as a person, and not as a mere influence or force. To lie to the Holy Spirit (Acts 5:3), to grieve the Holy Spirit of God (Eph. 4:30), are expressions which imply a person who is pleased or displeased. In no sense can they be made to refer to something impersonal.

The book of Acts contains many allusions to the personal leading of the Spirit. He said to Philip, 'Go to that chariot and stay near it' (8:29). He spoke to Peter (10:19), and to Paul and Barnabas (13:2). The Jerusalem Council said, 'It seemed good to the Holy Spirit and to us' (Acts 15:28) – language which could not have been used if the Holy Spirit were nothing but an influence.

Collecting together the evidence supplied by Scripture, we may put the arguments for the personality of the Spirit under six headings:

1. Personal actions are ascribed to Him (John 14:26; 1 Cor. 12:11).

2. He is personally distinguished from the Father and the Son, as is His mission (John 15:26).

3. Equal status and power belong to Him together with the Father and the Son (Matt. 28:19; 2 Cor. 13:14).

4. His appearance in a visible form at the baptism of Christ (Matt. 3:16) and on the day of Pentecost (Acts 2:3).

5. The sin against the Holy Spirit implies that He is personal (Matt. 12:31).

6. He is distinguished from His gifts (1 Cor. 12:11).

We need to remember, however, that the full evaluation of the person and work of the Holy Spirit in connection with the Church is still future. At present His work is unseen and incomplete. The personality and deity of the Spirit will, however, one day be displayed in conspicuous glory when He completes the marvellous transformation of the Church of Jesus Christ (Rom. 8:20-23).

The procession of the Holy Spirit
The words of Christ on which this discussion largely turns are the following:

> 'When the Counsellor comes, whom I will send to you from the Father, the Spirit of truth who goes out (or proceeds) from the Father, he will testify about me' (John 15:26).

From this verse, three things challenge our attention:

1. The Spirit was sent by Christ from the Father.

2. The relationship was prior to that sending, on which that sending rests ('who proceeds from the Father').

3. The present tense – 'proceeds' – indicates a continuous action.

In Scripture the Spirit is called: the Spirit of the Lord (Isa. 11:2); the Spirit of God (Rom. 8:9); the Spirit who proceeds from the Father (John 15:26); the Spirit of His Son (Gal. 4:6).

All of these titles clearly indicate 'procession' – that the Spirit proceeds, goes out, goes forth from the Father and the Son.

The deity of the Holy Spirit
The supreme deity of the Holy Spirit is clearly established by the procession of the Spirit. Just as we say that the only Son is the supreme God, not although He is the Son, but because He was begotten by the Father; so we may say that the Spirit is supreme God, not although, but because He proceeds from the Father and the Son.

We offer the following five proofs for the supreme deity of the Holy Spirit:

1. The divine acts of creation and providence are attributed to the Spirit (Gen. 1:2; Ps. 33:6; Job 26:13). Creation and providence are clearly the work of the supreme God alone. All that creative and conserving power is ascribed to the Spirit of God.

2. Divine attributes are ascribed to Him. We may select for our consideration two attributes in particular: omniscience (He is all-knowing) and omnipresence (He is everywhere present).

   We find omniscience ascribed to the Spirit when it is said: 'God has revealed it to us by his Spirit. The Spirit searches all things, even the deep things of God... no-one knows the thoughts of God except the Spirit of God.' (1 Cor. 2:10, 11).

   We find omnipresence ascribed to the Spirit in Psalm 139:7: 'Where can I go from your Spirit? Where can I flee from your presence?'.

3. Divine honours and worship are given to Him. This is perhaps best revealed by the declaration that the sin against the Holy Spirit can never be forgiven. This could not be affirmed unless the Holy Spirit had divine dignity and status.

4. The equal status He is given with the Father and the Son. For example, at the baptism of Christ (Matt. 3:16, 17); the outpouring of the Spirit at Pentecost (Acts 2:33); the fact that through Christ we have access by the Spirit to the Father (Eph. 2:18).

Perhaps the best example of all is in 2 Corinthians 13:14: 'May the grace of the Lord Jesus Christ, and the love of God, and the fellowship of the Holy Spirit be with you all'. It is as if Paul were saying: 'O Lord Jesus Christ, let your grace; O Father, let your love; O Holy Spirit, let the communication of yourself be with them all.' The equal status of the Spirit is clearly indicated.

5. The name of God is given to Him indirectly. There are clear instances where He who is called the Holy Spirit in one clause is called God in another, e.g. Acts 5:3, 4, and compare Psalm 95:7, 8 with Hebrews 3:7.

Throughout this chapter we have chiefly established the personality and divine nature of the Holy Spirit by inference. Why does the Bible not use explicit statements more often? As Lampe has happily put it: 'It is fitting that he who speaks by all the prophets and apostles (in Scripture), as his scribes, should speak less of himself, when the work itself abundantly commends the author.'

5.
The Holy Spirit and Jesus Christ

There are two major thoughts that confront us with reference to the identity of Christ throughout the Old and New Testament: (1) that He is a divine person, and (2) the anointed Servant of the Lord. On the one hand, the child born is designated as the Wonderful Counsellor, the Mighty God (Isa. 9:6); and, on the other hand, He is called the Servant of the Lord upon whom the Spirit rests (Isa. 42:1). And these two thoughts, though they may be distinguished, are never separated in biblical teaching.

There was a constant action of the Spirit on the humanity of Christ. His human nature was immediately and continually filled and led by the Spirit.

We must notice that, prior to Pentecost, the Bible speaks of the activity of the Spirit along with the Son. The Spirit had a part to play in the person and work of Christ.

1. Incarnation
The first stage of this anointing with the Spirit took place at the incarnation or birth of Christ: 'The Holy Spirit will come upon you, and the power of the Most High will overshadow you. So the holy one to be born will be called the Son of God' (Luke 1:35). These words show us that the Holy Spirit was the creator of Christ's sinless humanity.

The Lord's humanity was produced by the Holy Spirit in a supernatural way, and therefore did not contract guilt from Adam. No corruption of sin was transmitted to Him. Thus Christ was included in the human family (He was really human) and yet not included in its sinfulness. He was 'the last Adam' (1 Cor. 15:45).

The Holy Spirit was in Christ from the moment of conception, supplying Him with all the physical, intellectual and spiritual powers necessary for His great life work.

2. Ministry

The second stage of the giving of the Holy Spirit took place at Christ's baptism. This should be understood as the public inauguration of the Lord Jesus into His ministry, and it was the occasion of conferring upon Him the supernatural gifts which had been promised in Old Testament prophecy.

The Spirit given at the baptism was provided to equip Christ for the execution of His mediatorial work, as Prophet, Priest and King. Consequently, Christ spoke the words of God (as Prophet), and draws all His people to Himself by the power of the Holy Spirit (as King).

The next event in Christ's life was the temptation, of which it is said that He was 'led by the Spirit into the desert to be tempted' (Matt. 4:1). Christ's human nature was victorious throughout the whole assault by the sustaining power of the Holy Spirit. When the temptation was over, the account continues: 'Jesus returned to Galilee in the power of the Spirit' (Luke 4:14).

Another memorable fact was the sermon He preached in the synagogue of Nazareth, where He was well known (Luke 4:16). Here He read the words of Isaiah: 'The Spirit of the Sovereign LORD is on me, because the Lord has anointed me to preach' (Isa. 61:1). Then He added these breath-taking words: 'Today this scripture is fulfilled in your hearing' (Luke 4:21). His townsfolk wondered at the gracious words that came from His mouth as He spoke by the Spirit who had anointed Him.

The next fact which reveals that He acted by the Spirit was the casting out of Satan: 'If I drive out demons by the Spirit of God, then the kingdom of God has come upon you' (Matt. 12:28). The Lord Jesus was then face to face with the kingdom of Satan, and was setting up the kingdom of God. By the Spirit of God who rested on Him, He was able to work miracles in general, and to cast out Satan in particular from his fortress in the human heart. In this way, He showed that the King of a new kingdom was on the scene and had begun His reign over those who are born of the Spirit.

We next refer to the Spirit's activity in connection with the cross, which was Christ's priestly self-sacrifice. We read these words: 'who thorough the eternal Spirit offered himself unblemished to God' (Heb. 9:14). The meaning is, that the Son of God, motivated and strengthened by the Holy Spirit, offered Himself unblemished as an atoning sacrifice. It was the Holy Spirit who supplied the strength to go through with the dreadful ordeal to the end.

To the cross we add, of course, the resurrection, and here too, we discover the vital involvement of the Holy Spirit. Christ was raised from death by the Holy Spirit, as Peter teaches clearly in 1 Peter 3:18.

3. Exaltation

This is the third stage of the operation of the Holy Spirit in connection with Christ. It is described in Acts 2:33 in the following words: 'Exalted to the right hand of God, he has received from the Father the promised Holy Spirit and has poured out what you now see and hear'.

It follows that we may think of the promised Holy Spirit as a gift from the ascended Christ to His people.

Before His resurrection, Christ received the Spirit, and the Spirit's activity was mainly limited to the person of Christ. With His resurrection, the day came when He showed that the great result of His atoning death was the power of giving the Holy Spirit to others.

As Mediator, the Lord Jesus was anointed with the Holy Spirit for the fulfilment of all His functions and all His activity. The right to send the Holy Spirit into the hearts of fallen human beings was obtained by the atonement for sin which Christ made by His life and death.

There is a clear balance in the Bible between the Son and the Spirit. Neither is superior to the other. Sometimes, we read of the Son being dependent on the Spirit for direction and power; at other times, the Son is said to give the Spirit and to send the Spirit. It is clear that the Bible intends us to understand that there was a united mission in which the Son and the Spirit acted together for the salvation of believing men and women.

6.
The inspiration of the prophets and apostles

In the Old and New Testaments, we find two kinds of spiritual gift. First, the ordinary gifts for the salvation of God's people; secondly, the extraordinary (or supernatural) gifts for special service. It is the extraordinary gifts that we are concerned with in this chapter, and it is important to recognise from the outset that these gifts were temporary, not permanent.

From the earliest times, extraordinary gifts were given to those who received the word of God, first to Moses, through whom the law was first given, and then to the succession of prophets who spoke the word of God to their own generation, or wrote it, by God's command, for all the generations to come. The Spirit is referred to as the author of these supernatural gifts (Heb. 2:4), and they ceased when they were no longer needed for the great purpose for which they were given.

1. Prophets
This gift of prophecy was the chief gift of God in Old Testament times. Prophecy was not, as some think, mere religious enthusiasm, or a high religious conscience.

Revelation 19:10 refers to the Spirit as the spirit of Prophecy: 'For the testimony of Jesus is the spirit of prophecy'. This may also be translated 'the Spirit of prophecy is the testimony of Jesus'. This indicates to us that the Spirit spoke in all the prophets and, most importantly, that the scope or aim of all prophecy was to testify to Jesus (compare John 15:26).

The apostle Peter has some important words to say about prophecy: 'Prophecy never had its origin in the will of man, but men spoke from God as they were carried along by the Holy Spirit' (2 Pet. 1:21). They remained silent until they received the Spirit's communication. The Spirit did not give them this gift as a permanent possession, which they could use as and when they pleased. He so moved them that they could not but speak or write what the Spirit constrained them to declare.

2. Apostles

There were very many supernatural gifts in the New Testament Church, but they all culminated in the apostles, who were the instruments of Christ's revelation to the Church, and who were invested with a commission that extended to all lands and which lasts for all time. The Church is built on the apostles and will continue to stand on that foundation until the return of Christ.

As far as those supernatural gifts which the Spirit distributed amongst the apostles, and even to some outside that circle, are concerned, we should note that: these gifts were limited to individuals, and were not universal; they were temporary, so that one might possess them today and lack them tomorrow; and they were by no means co-extensive with the possession of divine grace. In other words, they did not necessarily accompany God's saving grace in an individual's life.

When, therefore, Scripture was completed (and therefore closed), these extraordinary gifts of the Spirit were no longer necessary. And these gifts did pass away then. Nor is the church warranted to expect their restoration, or to desire prophetic visions, immediate revelations, or miraculous gifts, either in public or in private, beyond or besides the all-perfect Scripture.

Those who long for, or expect, or claim such a restoration have not thought seriously about the greatness of the work of the Spirit in the provision and completion of the Holy Scriptures as a gift to the Church for all time.

The presence of miraculous gifts in both Old and New Testament times served a twofold purpose. Firstly, they were an undeniable proof of a supernatural revelation from God to man (Heb. 2:4). Secondly, they were a trustworthy sign of the inward miracle of inspiration.

Some would argue that these gifts have been lost through the fault of the Church and not the will of God, and that they could be restored to the believing expectation of the Church.

What use would the gifts be today? They were given to attest revelation, but revelation has now ceased and is complete in the Scriptures. Furthermore, had they been intended as the Church's permanent possession, they would not have been withheld for nearly two thousand years.

The statement on inspiration which I wish to put forward and defend is the following:

> The Holy Spirit gave prophets and apostles special gifts, which must be distinguished from ordinary saving grace, to give forth in human forms of speech a revelation which must be accepted as the word of God in its whole contents, and as the authoritative guide for belief and practice.

We must keep in mind the twofold character of revelation. Revelation exists both as fact and as word. The act comes first – the revelation of the Son of God; the word follows. The event is explained by the word. In the New Testament the revelation is comprised of the historical facts of the incarnation, atonement and resurrection of Christ, and also of the perfect narrative or record of these facts in the written word.

Of this written word, the Holy Spirit is the author. And the Spirit gave His revelation in human forms of speech. This was a condescension on the Spirit's part. Indeed, it is not unsuitable to say that, as God is said to humble Himself to look upon the things on the earth (Ps. 113:6), and as the Son humbled Himself when He became obedient to death (Phil. 2:8), so the Holy Spirit humbles Himself in giving His message – no matter how great and high its content – in a form of speech which often resembles a mother's accommodation to the capacity of an infant. And this was necessary so that the written word might easily pass into the speech and writing of every language in the world.

The Spirit graciously speaks to man, first to prophets and apostles, and through them to all men, not in an elevated style, not communicating only ideas above the range of most people or merely for cultured or philosophical minds, but He speaks in easy, clear language, suited to the understanding of everyone.

However, we do not say that we know how the Spirit inspired prophets and apostles. The writers were not mere machines, or like secretaries taking a dictated letter. Scripture itself, with that reticence which is one of its unique features, never discloses the mode of the Holy Spirit in inspiration. This whole matter is enveloped in mystery. We should not attempt to define the undefinable. It was a miracle. Nevertheless, we affirm with all our hearts the fact and the reality of inspiration.

The analogy between the person of Christ and the Scriptures has often been used and is indeed useful. The two natures, divine and human, in the one person of Christ, are there and they work together to the same end, but it is not possible to say where the one nature begins and the other ends in Christ's great work of redemption. So it is with the Scriptures; they are at once and inseparably divine and human.

It is most important for us to distinguish 'inspiration' from 'illumination'. In other words, the Spirit's original revelation to prophets and apostles is of a different (and higher) order to our reception of this revelation (by the same Spirit). The important point is this: the prophets and apostles were uniquely acted upon by the Spirit as He commanded to them the revelation of God.

In conclusion, I wish to say something about the testimony or witness of the Holy Spirit to the Scriptures. We must not consider this an operation of the Spirit apart from the Scriptures themselves, as some have done. Rather, this is an activity of the Spirit by and through the Scriptures themselves. The Spirit and the words of God work together, not separately. Just as the sun is seen by its own light, Scripture is known by its own light and the power of the Holy Spirit.

7.
Regeneration

Regeneration refers to the application of redemption to the individual. This is the particular activity of God the Holy Spirit. It is based on and it brings to fulfilment the personal election of God the Father and the redemption of God the Son.

Before regeneration, the human condition may be summarised in these three statements:

1) A lack of the Spirit and all spiritual life (Eph. 2:1).
2) Slavery to the kingdom of sin and of Satan (John 8:34).
3) Voluntary aversion to God and rebellion against Him (Rom. 8:7).

Correspondingly, we shall discover:

1) How the Spirit is restored to the human heart.
2) How people are transferred from the family of Satan to the family of God.
3) How that sinful nature is transformed.

The first two of these will be discovered in this chapter, the third in the next chapter.

The restoration of the Spirit

How does the Spirit return to the human heart? He does so solely on the basis of the redemption achieved by Jesus Christ.

Man, in his natural (fallen) state, is no longer a spiritual being, and it is incorrect to speak of him in that way. Instead, the Bible describes man as not having the Spirit, unspiritual (Jude 19; 1 Cor. 2:14). His wisdom, or way of thinking is 'earthly' (James 3:15), and he is 'without God' (Eph. 2:12).

The fact of human inability, which Scripture everywhere asserts or implies, is to be explained by the withdrawal of the Spirit, which has left men and women in spiritual death.

Perhaps the most important passage concerning this activity of the Spirit is found in John 16:8-11. Three aspects of this activity are mentioned here.

In the first place, the Holy Spirit convinces the world about sin – the sin of unbelief, the rejection of Christ and His gospel. This is the greatest sin of all because it leaves all guilt remaining, it gives power to existing sin, and it is the origin of a polluted conscience. Secondly, the Holy Spirit convinces the world about righteousness. That is, the Holy Spirit convinces people of their great need for the righteousness of Christ to cover their own unrighteousness. Thirdly, the Holy Spirit convinces the world about judgement. That is, the judgement of Satan by Christ. Christ has overcome Satan, so that His people may be set free from Satan.

What is this convincing process that Christ speaks of in John's Gospel? It can be nothing other than the process of conversion itself, the process which makes a person a Christian.

Christ speaks of a sin against the Holy Spirit which cannot be forgiven. What is this sin? There have been differing views on the subject by notable Christians. I tend to agree with Augustine of the early church who understood it to be the failure to repent and trust in Christ.

But in regeneration, the Spirit works on the person's mind, will and conscience. He opens the mind to understand spiritual truth. He strengthens the will to obey Christ. He corrects, teaches, cleanses and strengthens the conscience daily.

Adoption into the family of God

Those who are called by the Holy Spirit become adopted children and are transferred by His power from the family of Satan into the family of God.

It is not correct to say that God is the Father of all people, as some like to say. He is not the Father of those who do not trust in Christ. In fact, as Christ Himself said, they belong to a family antagonistic to the family of God and follow their father, the devil (John 8:44).

The great privilege of adoption must be distinguished from the great privilege of justification. We not only become legally just and right with God (justification), but we enter into a new relationship with God as a child with a father (adoption).

In Romans 8:16 Paul teaches that there is assurance of adoption from the Spirit of adoption. This 'testimony' or 'witness' of the Spirit is not spoken of as the privilege of only certain believers, but as a common Christian experience. However, it does not follow that a Christian believer will always enjoy a full assurance. It is right to seek assurance at all times, but it is not right to say that someone who does not always enjoy assurance cannot be a real Christian, nor to think so of ourselves.

It is vital for us to understand that it is the Spirit alone who causes conversion. We contribute nothing towards it. It was the Lord Jesus Himself who said that the new birth (which is the work of the Holy Spirit) is the essential feature of Christianity (John 3:3). In fact, so indispensable is it, that without it there can be no spiritual health or progress, nor any interest in Christ and His benefits.

The gift of the Spirit does not come after, but before someone believes in Christ. Indeed, there would be no faith if the Spirit did not come first to provide it. Many incorrectly put these the other way round. But the Spirit comes first, then faith.

The regenerating activity of the Spirit comes before human responses to the gospel, not after. The very first desire, resolution or prayer we have for the gospel is from the Holy Spirit. The simple but vitally important thing to remember is this: all spiritual good comes from the Spirit of God.

It follows that the application of redemption to the human being is, from first to last, by the Holy Spirit. The faith exercised by the human person is a gift from the Spirit of God.

The Bible very clearly teaches that man is powerless, indeed dead, in his sin. He is entirely unable to contribute anything towards his spiritual awakening. That awakening is one hundred per cent the activity of the Holy Spirit. So all the credit, all the glory and all the gratitude belong to the Holy Spirit.

Regeneration is a very powerful work. It is compared in the Bible to creation (Ps. 51:10; Eph. 2:10), and to resurrection (Eph. 1:19). Such work can only be God's work.

8.
The Spirit of holiness

In this chapter we move on from that activity of the Spirit which initiates the Christian life (previous chapter) to that activity which continues and develops the Christian life. The first activity is called 'regeneration', the second 'sanctification', which means the process by which a person becomes increasingly holy.

We begin by recalling that most important principle of Christian religion, the inseparable connection between the work of Christ for us and the work of the Spirit in us. In other words, the inseparable connection between justification (the work of Christ for us) and sanctification (the work of the Spirit in us).

There are now two vital things for us to consider in relation to the activity of the Holy Spirit in sanctification. First, the union created by the Holy Spirit between Christ and the Christian. Secondly, the permanent residence of the Holy Spirit in the Christian.

The Bible uses picture-language to describe the reality of union with Christ: marriage, the head and the body, the vine and the branches, the temple and the cornerstone. There is, then, the most intimate relationship between Christ and the Christian, and the Christian experiences many powerful effects of this union in his life. Thanks to this connection, Christ's Spirit, Christ's holiness and Christ's joy flow over into our lives.

The second great reality is that the Spirit of God Himself comes to live permanently in all true Christians. This is taught in very many places in the Bible – John 14:16; 2 Timothy 1:14; 1 Corinthians 3:16; 2 Corinthians 6:16; Ephesians 2:22. In all these passages the Holy Spirit is said to occupy the Christian's heart as His temple, pervading and enlivening all the powers of the Christian's mind. This is what underlies all the Christian's holiness and growth.

Overall, we may think of the Spirit's presence in four different ways:

First, there is a universal presence of the Spirit in all the wide realms of creation for the conservation of all things.

Secondly, there is a special sanctifying presence, where the Spirit lives in true Christians throughout life and death and until they reach heaven.

Thirdly, there is His presence in the Son of God, Jesus Christ, divine and human (which we have earlier considered).

Fourthly, there is His presence in glorified Christians, that is those who are now in heaven.

In this chapter, we are concerned with the second of these.

It is very important for us to recognise a distinction between the activity of the Spirit in regeneration and His subsequent activity in sanctification, in other words, before and after conversion. In regeneration, there was no co-operation involved between the Spirit and the individual person. But in sanctification, co-operation is required. Sanctification is not an automatic process. It does not just happen in the

Christian life. The Christian is now able, and is now required, to co-operate actively with the Holy Spirit in the process that makes the Christian increasingly holy.

What makes Christian morality different from all other views of morality is the fact that it is not pursued to earn salvation, but because the individual is already saved by grace. As the Bible puts it, the good tree produces good fruit; the fruit cannot change the tree. In other words, Christian morality is the result of the power of the Spirit, not the other way round.

Christians are able to achieve moral standards that others could never achieve, because they have the Spirit of holiness active within them. In fact, so great is the power within, that to a certain extent the Christian, in close fellowship with Christ, practises Christian qualities (Gal. 5:22-23) naturally and almost effortlessly. Christianity is vitalised by the Spirit of life. It is not influenced by a thought or an idea.

In addition to the power to live a new life, supplied by the Holy Spirit, the Christian has a great example to follow: the Lord Jesus Christ. Again, however, the activity of the Holy Spirit is vital. The imitation of Christ, or Christ-likeness, which is the aim of the Christian life, cannot for a moment take place apart from the power of the Spirit. The Christian becomes like Christ as he considers Christ, as he sees the glory of Christ, in the word of God by the enlightenment of the Holy Spirit. The Holy Spirit alone makes transformation into the image of Christ a possibility and a reality.

There have, however, been some misunderstandings of the activity of the Holy Spirit in the Christian's life, which we must now point out.

One misunderstanding is that, by the power of the Holy Spirit, the Christian can become perfect in this life. The Bible (and Christian experience), however, clearly teach that this is not possible. In fact, we find that all Christians are commonly ready to acknowledge how far they are from the great goal for which Christ has taken hold of them. Perfection is always the aim, but never the attainment of the Christian life. Even Paul the apostle had not arrived, however much he forgot the things behind him, and reached for the things before him (Phil. 3:13).

There have also been some who have taught that it is possible for the Christian in this life to do the will of God without any inward opposition or conflict. However, the experience of the Christian plainly teaches otherwise, as is clearly brought out by Paul in Romans 7:14-25. Paul is here describing his own experience as a Christian (and not before he became a Christian) as Augustine and all the Reformers have clearly demonstrated. Paul was writing of the conflict taking place within his own soul at the time when he wrote the letter to the Romans.

The apostle Paul draws a distinction between his true self and the sin that lives in him. Not that he should escape personal responsibility for his sin in this way, but in order to rise above the dejection of such a constant, unrelenting conflict.

We feel an inner resistance whenever we engage in any spiritual activity because of the sin which remains in us. It is similar to the effort required to move a broken arm. In the same way, any spiritual activity is met by opposition from its enemy in us.

We draw to a close with this conclusion: while the Spirit of holiness is continually active within us, the degree to which believers achieve holiness is always imperfect and defective. While Christians press towards the goal, they are never perfect, nor do they ever reach a stage in this life where there is no more conflict, and no performance of God's will without the consciousness of inward opposition.

9.
The Church

In this final chapter, we explore the Spirit's work in the church, first in founding the Church, and then in His activity in and through the Church and its sacraments.

The Church of Christ did not, properly speaking, exist during Old Testament days on earth, although there were individual believers at that time. It was at Pentecost that the Lord, by the power of His Spirit, welded into a Church those individual believers.

The activity of the Spirit is essential to the existence and the whole life of the Church. The Church has come into existence by the election of the Father, the redemption of the Son, and the regeneration of the Holy Spirit. The Spirit creates the Church, sustains and supports it, provides life, power and gifts so that its members can strengthen one another. By the Holy Spirit every true member is spiritually joined to Christ, the Head of the Church, and by the Holy Spirit true members of Christ's Church are spiritually joined to one another.

How does the activity of the Holy Spirit in the Church agree with the biblical teaching that Christ is Head and Lord of the Church? There is no tension, but only harmony. The Lord Jesus, the Mediator, teaches, rules and guides His Church by the Holy Spirit. Christ does everything by the Spirit. There is no competition involved. The exalted Christ continuously acts for the Church's good by His Spirit through the Scriptures.

The Church has a twofold function, and we must neglect neither function. It exists both as a holy community and as a missionary enterprise.

A holy community

The Church is first of all a united community. Paul says, 'There is one body and one Spirit' (Eph. 4:4). Throughout the ages and throughout the world, the Church is one community under one Head, knit together by the Holy Spirit. The Church is not one because of its own efforts to create unity for itself but because its members share the one Spirit. The Church is a temple in which God lives by His Spirit, the believers being joined together like stones in a building (see Eph. 2:19-22 and 1 Pet. 2:4-5).

To this holy community, to His Church, Christ has given two sacraments[5]: baptism and the Lord 's Supper. It is the Spirit who makes these sacraments effective. We reject the view of Roman Catholicism that these sacraments possess power and grace in themselves. On the other hand, we also reject the view (associated with Zwingli) that the sacraments are merely empty signs.

John Calvin taught the middle way, which is the biblical way. On the one hand, the sacraments do not impart grace of themselves automatically (there is no 'grace' in the water, bread or wine themselves). On the other hand, nor are the sacraments mere 'empty' signs. They are channels of grace to every believing recipient. This grace comes from the Holy Spirit.

---

[5] 'sacrament': an outward and visible sign and symbol of an inward and spiritual grace.

A missionary enterprise

In addition to gathering people into the Church of Christ and building them up in the Church, it is the Spirit who gives the Church power to proclaim the gospel to others.

The rich supply of supernatural and extraordinary gifts given at Pentecost was not intended to continue when they had served their purpose in founding the Christian Church. The other gifts of an 'ordinary' character (preaching especially) were given for the permanent benefit of the Church, and are so essential to her spiritual life and growth that without them, the Church would collapse or disappear. The fact that they continue is a constant proof that Christ lives as the giver of the Holy Spirit

The first disciples were told to wait for the power of the Holy Spirit; and for us this is an example we are always to follow. Before the Spirit came we find the disciples ignorant, timid and proud. When the Spirit came there was no more debate about who should be the greatest. They became changed men.

In the Church we find the greatest apparent opposites: weakness and power, emptiness and sufficiency, limitation and the boundless resources of God's power; the jar of clay (2 Cor. 4:7) ready to fall to pieces at the slightest pressure and the greatness of His power; what the prophets calls the worm Jacob threshing the mountains and beating them small (Isa. 41:14-15).

We now turn our attention to the Spirit's activity in a revival, when an extraordinarily large number of people become Christians all at one time.

The work of the Spirit, wherever it occurs, needs to be distinguished from the things that accompany it and from the counterfeits that may be expected. Many things occur in a revival which all too clearly prove that it is necessary not only to pray for revival, but also for wisdom equal to the occasion when it occurs. If a revival is not produced by God's truth, it will be little more than a moment of excitement stirred up by human methods.

There is a certain kind of preaching associated with a revival. It is the kind that urges an immediate response of faith and repentance to the gospel of Jesus Christ. This is accompanied by the further statement that without the Holy Spirit, human beings cannot respond. They must, but they cannot. Responsibility, but inability. At this point this preaching drives home with overwhelming force. It compels action and dependence. As George Whitfield said, referring to the effects of this style of American preaching, 'After they have done all, God may deny them mercy.'

There is also a particular kind of praying during a revival. The Christian community is waiting, just as the original disciples waited at Pentecost, for the great outpouring of the Spirit. No other way is prescribed for us, and the Church has all the warrant she ever had to wait, expect and pray. The first disciples waited in simple hope, not for a Spirit they had nothing of, but for more of the Spirit they already had. And that should be the Church's attitude still. The more the Church waits for the Spirit and asks for His grace, the more we receive.[6]

---

[6] Smeaton ends with a footnote from Foster on prayer, which is well worth including here:

'I am convinced that everyone who is convinced of his dependence on God, which is a fact for everyone, will find himself impelled to pray, and will be concerned to persuade his friends to pray, almost every hour. He needs prayer like a sailor needs wind in his sails… If all, or even most, Christians, would pray like this, they would turn the world upside-down'.

PART TWO.
Fellowship with the Holy Spirit
(John Owen)

10.
The basis of our fellowship
with the Holy Spirit

The basis of all our fellowship with the Holy Spirit is explained by the Lord Jesus in John 16:1-7. He is going to leave His disciples. He knows that they are deeply saddened by that fact. 'All this I have told you so that you will not go astray' (v. 1). 'I have', He says, 'told you in advance the things you will suffer in case you had expected something else and throw away your faith. Now, you have been forewarned, and know what to expect. You will be persecuted, you may even be killed.'

'This is devastating', they might reply, 'do you mean that men, by killing us, will think they are doing a service to God?' 'Yes, they will', says the Saviour, 'and yet, so that you may not be mistaken, know that their blind and desperate ignorance is the cause of their fury and persuasion'. According to verse 3: 'They will do such things because they have not known the Father or me'.

This then is the situation of the disciples. But why did our Saviour tell it to them at this time, adding fear and confusion to their grief and sorrow? What advantage would they have from this knowledge? He explains in verse 4 that there are important reasons why He should tell them these things; primarily, that they would be prepared, so that when these things did take place their minds would be supported with the knowledge that He was God and He knew all things – having told them these things before they happened. 'I have told you this, so that when the time comes you will remember that I warned you' (v. 4).

Then they might have replied – but if it was so important, why did not you tell us earlier? Why not at the beginning, when you first called us to become your disciples? 'Just because', says our Saviour, 'there was no need to do so; for when I was with you, you had my protection and direction at hand. I did not tell you this at first because I was with you' (v. 4b).

'But now your situation has changed', He goes on, 'and I must leave you. For your part', He says, 'you are so overwhelmed with sorrow that you do not even think to ask Me where I am going – if you did you would surely be comforted, for I am going to be glorified and to carry out the work of your salvation, but your hearts are filled with sorrow and fears, and you do not even seek comfort' (vv. 5, 6). And then He adds that wonderful statement: 'But I tell you the truth: It is for your good that I am going away. Unless I go away, the Counsellor will not come to you; but if I go, I will send him to you' (v. 7).

This verse then (v. 7), being the very foundation of what we are about to consider, must now be considered in detail.

1. The preface of this verse

  (a) The first word 'But' (Greek '*alla*') is designed to lessen their fears, not to lessen anything He has just said. 'I know you have sad thoughts about these things, but…' He is about to tell them why they can be glad rather than sad!

(b) 'I tell you the truth' – the words are emphatic and anticipate something of great importance. He says 'I' – 'I tell it to you; I who love you, who take care of you, who am now about to lay down My life for you; they are My dying words, that you may believe Me; I who am truth itself, I tell you.'

'I tell you the truth' – You have in your sad, misgiving hearts many misapprehensions. You think that if only I would stay with you, all these evils would be prevented – but you do not know what is good for you, nor what is right. 'I tell you the truth' – this is truth itself, calm your heart in it.

There is need of a great deal of truth-telling, to comfort their souls, so dejected by the thought that He was about to leave them, whether their apprehension was right or wrong. And this was the first part of the Saviour's address to them, to free their minds from prejudice, and to prepare them to receive that great truth He was about to give them.

2. The assertion made in the verse

'It is for your good that I go away'. There are two things to note in these words: Christ's departure and the advantage of it to His disciples.

(a) By His departure He means the withdrawing of His physical presence from the earth after His resurrection – 'to remain in heaven until the time comes for God to restore everything' (Acts 3:21). As far as His deity was concerned He had promised to be with them to the end of the world (Matt. 28:20).

(b) About this departure He said, 'It is for your good, for your advantage'. This then is what the Saviour asserts

65

so emphatically to convince His followers of the truth of it – namely that His departure, which they so much feared and were troubled even to think about, would turn to their good and advantage.

3. The coming of the Comforter

Christ expresses Himself negatively and positively: 'If I do not go away, he will not come; but if I go away, I send him'.

He calls the Holy Spirit (Greek '*parakletos*'). This word has two meanings in particular: 'advocate' and 'comforter'. The Holy Spirit is revealed as both – for the disciples' trouble and sorrow, a Comforter; for advancing the cause of Christ against the world (v., 8), an Advocate. We will use the title 'Comforter'.

The sorrow of the disciples requires the Comforter. The Lord Jesus says to them, 'Sorrow has filled your hearts, but I will send you the Comforter'.

Who this Comforter is, Christ has already declared. He is 'the Spirit of truth' (John 15:26), the Holy Spirit who reveals all truth to men and women.

About Him, two things are affirmed:

(a) that He will come, and
(b) that Christ will send Him.

(a) The Holy Spirit will come as a result of Christ's departure. Christ says 'if I do not go, he will not come; but if I do go, he will come'. There is not only the sending of the Spirit by Christ, but the Spirit's own determination in this respect – 'he will come'.

(b) 'I will send him.' Christ teaches His disciples gradually about His sending the Spirit. Chapter 14:16: 'I will ask the Father and he will give you another Counsellor to be with you for ever'. Then He goes a step further in verse 26: 'But the Counsellor, the Holy Spirit, whom the Father will send in my name'; but in chapter 15:26 He says, 'I will send him'. The matter of sending the Holy Spirit by Christ was a deep mystery, which they could not take in all at once, so He teaches them gradually.

Here is a summary of the above:
The presence of the Holy Spirit with believers as a Comforter, sent by Christ, is better for believers than any physical presence of Christ Himself can be, now that Christ has completed His sacrifice on the cross for sin.

4. Now the Holy Spirit is sent for a twofold purpose
As a Spirit of sanctification for the elect, to convert them and make them believers, and as a Spirit of encouragement for believers, to give them all the good things that come from the death and redemption of Christ.

5. The source of the sending of the Spirit is the Father, from His electing love
This is the order of the operations: first there is the purpose of His love, the source of everything; then the asking of the Son (John 14:16), taking into account the merit of His righteousness and redemption; then follows the willing procession of the Holy Spirit.

The Holy Spirit both comes of His own accord, and is sent by the Father and the Son. There are three things to consider concerning this sending.

    (a) He is sent freely. He is 'given' (John 14:16). There are many other passages in the Bible that speak of the Spirit as a gift, e.g. 'he will give the Holy Spirit to those who ask him' (Luke 11:13). He is a gift and therefore 'free'.

The Spirit of grace is given by grace – given freely to regenerate and to encourage believers. For this reason He is said to be received through the gospel and not through the law (Gal. 3:2) – that is, by grace alone and not by our own acquirement. And all the Holy Spirit's operations are called 'free donations' (Greek '*charismata*'). He is freely given and He freely works. And in this way He is to be regarded, and to be asked for, and to be received. And we rejoice in the Comforter – that He is willing to come to us, and willing to be given to us. All of which highlights the grace of God.

(b) He is sent on the authority of the Father and the Son: the Father will send Him in Christ's name (John 14:26) and Christ will send Him (John 15:26).

There is here, in a very special way, the condescension and agreement of the Holy Spirit, in His love to us, to the authoritative delegation of the Father and the Son in this matter. This argues not for inequality of being (the Spirit is of the same divine essence as the Father and the Son), but simply for a difference of function.

It is for this reason that the sin against the Holy Spirit is unforgivable, having that quality of rebellion that no other sin has – because He comes not in His own name alone, though He does come in His own name, but in the name and authority of the Father and Son, from and by whom He is sent. And therefore to sin against Him is to sin against all the authority of God, all the love of the Trinity, and the deepest condescension of each person to fulfil the work of our salvation.

On this account we are to pray to the Father and the Son to give the Spirit to us. See Luke 11:13 – 'how much more will your Father in heaven give the Holy Spirit to those who ask him.' Now the Holy Spirit, being God, is no less to be prayed to, and called on, than the Father and Son. Why then do we ask the Father for Him, as we do in all our prayers, seeing that we also pray that He Himself would come to us and stay with us? In our prayers, we consider the Spirit as God over all, blessed for evermore; we pray for Him from the Father and the Son. And indeed, we are (as Christians generally do) to overflow with prayers, not only to the person of the Holy Spirit, but more appropriately to the Father and Son for the Spirit.

For this reason, there is a great importance laid on our not grieving the Spirit (Eph. 4:30) – because He comes in the name, with the love, and by the condescension of the whole divine Trinity.

The Holy Spirit is said not only to be given and sent, but also, in biblical terminology, to be poured out on us (e.g. Titus 3:6). And this was how the Old Testament often expressed the giving of the Spirit – the mystery of the Trinity not yet being fully revealed. See Isaiah 32:15: 'till the Spirit is poured upon us from on high, and the desert becomes a fertile field, and the fertile field seems like a forest.' That is, till the Gentiles be called to faith, and the Jews rejected. Other references include Isaiah 44:3 and Zechariah. 12:10. This expression is taken from the comparison of the Spirit with water.

This threefold expression – of giving, sending and pouring out of the Spirit – gives us the three great characteristics of the covenant of grace: first, that it is free (He is given); second, that it is orderly and sure, from the love of the Father, by the procurement of the Son; third, that it is effective.

We need now to make a biblical distinction between how we receive the Spirit as the Spirit of regeneration and how we receive the Spirit as the Spirit of encouragement.

(c) Our receiving of the Spirit as the Spirit of regeneration is a mere passive reception, as a container receives water. He comes as the wind on Ezekiel's dead bones, and makes them live; He comes into dead hearts, and revives them, by an act of His almighty power.

(d) However, with the Spirit of encouragement, it is different. Christians can receive the Spirit actively in this respect. And this is the power of faith. So in Galatians 3:2 they receive the Spirit by the hearing of faith – the preaching of the gospel, creating faith in them, enabled them to receive the Spirit. Thus, believing is put as the qualification for all our receiving of the Holy Spirit. John 7:39: 'he meant the Spirit, whom those who believed in him were later to receive.' It is believers who receive the Spirit, and they receive Him by faith. Faith perceives the promise of God and of Jesus Christ, of sending the Spirit for all those purposes for which He is given – therefore it depends, waits, relies on the promise, until it receives Him.

And He is received by prayer. He is given as the Spirit of prayer, so that we may ask for Him as the Spirit of encouragement (Luke 11:13); and indeed this asking for the Spirit of God, in the name of Christ, is the primary action of faith in this world.

6. The next important thing to consider is His stay with us
How does the Holy Spirit stay with us? It is by inhabitation or living within us. He lives within us chiefly as the Spirit of sanctification. He will be 'with you for ever' (John 14:16). We must go into this in a little more detail.

(a) He is promised to live with Christians for ever, in contrast to Christ who was with His disciples for only a few years. Christ, in the body, had been with them for a little while, and now was leaving them and returning to His Father. He had been the Comforter Himself for a time, but is now about to leave. They may have feared that this other Comforter would also be with them for only a short time. 'But no', says our Saviour, 'Do not be anxious; this is the last period. When I am gone, the Comforter is to do all the remaining work: there is not another to be expected, and I promise you him; nor shall he leave you, but always be with you.'

(b) The Comforter may always be with us, but may not always comfort us. He does not always do that work. For other purposes He is always with us: to make us holy. This was the case with David: 'Do not take your Holy Spirit from me' (Ps. 51:11-12). The Holy Spirit of sanctification was still with David, but he says, 'Restore to me the joy of your salvation'. Here he is referring to the Spirit of encouragement. He does not mean that the Spirit of holiness can leave him.

(c) There are times we refuse to be comforted! The offer is made, but refused. 'My soul refused to be comforted,' said David (Ps. 77:2).

(d) The Holy Spirit never leaves a Christian without any comfort and encouragement. Someone may well be

71

troubled, confused, refuse comfort – actually find none – but believers always have the source of comfort, which in time they will draw upon. Therefore, when God promises that He will heal sinners, and restore comfort to them, as in Isaiah 57:18, it is not because they were without any hope of being comforted.

Thus the Spirit, being sent and given, remains with the souls of believers. He does not leave them, though He reveals Himself to them in different ways – which is our subject for the next chapter.

11.
How the Holy Spirit works in us

What does the Holy Spirit do within us? How does He act in our lives?

1. He works effectively
1 Corinthians 12:11, 'All these are the work of one and the same Spirit'. And what He does, He does as God. His work must therefore be effective.

2. He distributes spiritual gifts to everyone just as He determines
He does so in complete freedom and with perfect wisdom. Thus Christians are kept in complete dependence on Him. He distributes as He determines (1 Cor. 12:7-11) – then who should not be content with his or her share? What claim can anyone lay to those works which He distributes by His own decision?

3. He gives
They 'began to speak in other tongues as the Spirit enabled them', (Acts 2:4). He gave the tongues to them, freely, as a gift. He can act freely because in the work of our salvation, the action of one person in the Trinity in no way interferes with the freedom of any other – so the love of the Father in sending

the Son is free, and in no way does this sending prejudice the freedom and love of the Son, but He lays down His life freely. In the same way, the redemption of the Son in no way affects the freedom of the Father's grace in forgiving and accepting us through Christ; and again, the Father and Son's sending of the Spirit does not detract from the freedom of the Spirit in His operations, but what He gives believers He gives freely. This is because the purpose of the Father, Son and Holy Spirit is essentially one and the same, so that in the work of one there is the free participation of all three.

12.
The work of the Holy Spirit

In this chapter we deal with the work of the Holy Spirit, and therefore how we have fellowship with the Holy Spirit.

1. He teaches and reminds

His teaching is included under the subject of anointing (see section 7 of this chapter), so we deal only with His work of reminding in detail here.

Our Saviour here promises His apostles that the Holy Spirit would bring to their minds the things He had said, so that by His inspiration they would be enabled to write and preach them for the good of his church. So Peter tells us, 'men spoke from God as they were carried along by the Holy Spirit', that is, in writing Scripture (2 Pet. 1:21). They were carried beyond themselves to speak His words. The apostles forgot much of what Christ said to them, and what they did retain was not enough to provide a foundation for faith to the church. So Christ promises the Holy Spirit for this work, so that the apostles might be able to pass on infallibly what He had said to them.

Christ was also promising His apostles that the Spirit would apply His words for their comfort and encouragement. He knew they were unable to make use of His words of comfort and so He was promising that the Spirit would bring them to their minds in full strength and vigour. And this is one reason why it was for good that Christ's bodily presence be substituted by the presence of the Spirit. Whilst Christ was with them, His promises made little impact on their hearts. But when the Spirit came, He filled those promises with power and His apostles with joy. That was the Holy Spirit's special work, and it is His work to the end of the world – to bring the promises of Christ to our minds and hearts, to give us the comfort of them, the joy and sweetness of them. It makes sense that these words follow: 'Peace I leave with you; my peace I give you' (John 14:27). The Comforter was sent to bring what Christ said to memory, and the consequence of that is peace, and freedom from a troubled heart – whatever peace, relief, comfort, joy, support we have at any time received from any promise or work of Christ, it is all due to the Comforter. It is only when He does this work that our natural abilities to call to mind and consider the promises of Christ become fully effective. And this work He does powerfully, voluntarily, and freely.

(a) He does it powerfully, and therefore comfort from the words and promises of Christ sometimes breaks in through all barriers into the saddest and darkest condition imaginable; it comes and makes men sing in a prison cell, rejoice in flames; it breaks in through temptations and the greatest distresses imaginable. Why is this? Because the Spirit is working, His power is in it, and nothing can stop it. If He decides to bring to our remembrance the promises of Christ for our encouragement, neither Satan, nor personal circumstances, nor sin, nor the world, nor death will interrupt our encouragement. This is something the Christian, who has fellowship with the Holy Spirit, knows to his advantage. Sometimes the skies seem black above us, and the earth seems to tremble beneath our feet; personal tragedies appear so full of horror and darkness that we are ready to collapse with the thought of them – but here is our great relief and the restoration of our souls; our comfort depends not on any outward condition or inward frame of mind, but on the powerful and effective action of the Holy Spirit, to which by faith they surrender themselves.

(b) He does it voluntarily – He distributes to each one just as He determines. For the same person, at one time he is full of joy and comfort in a time of great distress – every promise brings sweetness when his pressures are heavy. At another time, however, in the smallest trial he looks for comfort, searches out the promise, but it is far away. The reason for the difference is this – the Spirit distributes just as He determines. And it is so too with different people – for some, each promise is full of life and comfort, others however taste little all their days – again, because the Spirit distributes just as He determines. It all depends on the sovereign determination of the Holy Spirit.

(c) He does it freely. Much of the variety of this comforting with the promises of Christ depends on the freedom of the Spirit's working. For this reason, the comfort often comes unexpectedly, when the human heart has all the reasons in the world to expect distresses and sorrow.

And in this general work of the Holy Spirit towards us we have communion and fellowship with Him. No sooner does the soul begin to feel the life of a promise warming his heart, relieving, cherishing, supporting, delivering from fear and trouble, but it may, it must, know that the Holy Spirit is there – which knowledge will, in fact, add to the believer's joy, and lead into deeper fellowship with the Spirit.

2. He glorifies Christ

John 16:14: 'He will bring glory to me by taking from what is mine and making it known to you'. The work of the Spirit is to glorify Christ. The Spirit, coming as Christ's replacement, in no way competes with Christ for attention. On the contrary, He is devoted to bringing glory to Christ. A clear sign of a false spirit is that it does not glorify Christ, and there are many false spirits in the world.

He reveals to the souls of sinners the good things of the covenant of grace, provided by the Father, purchased by the Son. He shows to us mercy, grace, forgiveness, righteousness, acceptance with God; He lets us know that these are the things of Christ, procured by Christ for us; He shows them to us for our encouragement and strength. Then is Christ magnified and glorified in our hearts; then we know what a Saviour and Redeemer He is. 'No one can say, "Jesus is Lord," except by the Holy Spirit' (1 Cor. 12:3).

3. He pours out the love of God into our hearts (Rom. 5:5)

That is, the love of God for us, not our love for Him. The Comforter gives a sweet and abundant evidence and persuasion of the love of God to us, so that the human soul is delighted and fully satisfied.

This is His particular work. As all His works are works of love and kindness, so it is with this communication of the love of the Father. What experience we have of the spirit of heaven in this world arises from this love poured into our hearts.

4. He bears witness with our spirit that we are children of God (Rom. 8:16)

'The Spirit himself testifies with our spirit that we are God's children.' We know whose children we are by natural birth:

children of Satan and children of God's wrath. But by the Spirit we become part of another family, we are adopted as children of God, as we receive the Spirit of our Father.

The Christian is not always sure of this position, but the Spirit provides the reassurance. And in this He gives us holy fellowship with Himself. The soul knows His voice when He speaks. When the Lord Jesus Christ with one word stilled the raging of the sea and wind, all who were with Him knew there was divine power at hand (Matt. 8:25-27). And when the Holy Spirit with one word stills the turmoil and storms that arise in the soul, giving it an immediate calm and security, we know His divine power, and we can rejoice in His presence.

5. He seals us

Ephesians 1:13: 'Having believed, you were marked in him (Christ) with a seal, the promised Holy Spirit', and 'Do not grieve the Holy Spirit of God, with whom you were sealed for the day of redemption' (4:30).

With a seal, there are two things to be considered.

(a) the nature of the seal. The nature of the sealing involves the imparting of the image or character of the seal on to the thing sealed – to stamp the character of the seal on it.

(b) the purpose of the seal is twofold:

(i) To authenticate the contents.
The purpose is to make good and confirm what has been given, and when this is done it is irreversible. For this reason it is said that he who accepts the testimony of Christ 'has certified that God is truthful' (John 3:33).

(ii) To protect the contents.
People set seals on that which they wish to keep safe for themselves. In this sense the servants of God are said to

be sealed (Rev. 7:4) – that is, marked with God's mark, as His special people. Compare Ezekiel 9:4. This does not refer to something in the heart of the believer, but to the objective security of the believer – not to a *sense* of security, but to the *fact* of security. The Father gives His chosen people into the hands of Christ to be redeemed; having redeemed them, in due time they are called by the Spirit, and marked for God, and so surrender themselves into the hands of the Father.

6. He is our guarantee (2 Cor. 1:22; 5:5; Eph. 1:13-14)
Paul says He is a 'deposit'. A 'deposit' is part of the price of something given in advance to assure the person to whom it is given that at the agreed time the whole amount promised will be received.

Two things are required for a deposit:

(a) That it is part of the whole, of the same kind and nature as the whole, whether it is money or something else.

(b) That it is a confirmation of a promise. First, the whole thing is promised, then the deposit is given, to support the promise. The Spirit is this deposit, guaranteeing what is to come. God gives us the promise of eternal life. To confirm this to us, He gives us His Spirit – which is the first part of the promise, and assures us of the whole.

Moreover it is a guarantee in two respects.

(i) First of all, it is a guarantee in respect of God, in so far as God gives the Spirit as a part of the inheritance itself, and of the same kind as the whole, as a guarantee ought to. The full inheritance promised is the fullness of the Spirit in the enjoyment of God. When that Spirit which is given now in this world will have completely taken away all sin and sorrow, and will have made us able to enjoy the glory of God in His presence, that will be the full inheritance promised.

God does it for this purpose, to assure us of the inheritance. Having given us so many assurances 'outside' us – His word, His promises, His covenant, His oath, His revelation and the discovery of His faithfulness and changelessness in them all – He graciously also gives us an assurance within ourselves (Isa. 59:21), that we may have all the security we can have. What more can be done for us? He has given us the Holy Spirit, and in Him the first instalments of glory, the strongest pledge of His love, the guarantee of all our inheritance.

(ii) Secondly, it is a guarantee in respect of believers, in so far as He gives us an awareness of the love of God. He guarantees to believers that God is our Father and He will deal with us as with children. God sends His Spirit into our hearts crying 'Abba, Father', which means of course that we are not servants but sons, and if sons, then heirs of God.

He is the guarantee of the inheritance promised to believers – as Paul puts it, 'a deposit guaranteeing what is to come'. So He is in all respects a guarantee – given by God, received by us, as the beginning of our inheritance, and the assurance of it. As much as we have of the Spirit, that much we have of heaven in perfect enjoyment now and that much evidence of its future fullness. Every gracious, self-evidencing act of His life in the heart of the believer we rejoice in, as a drop from heaven, and we long for the whole ocean of it.

81

7. He anoints believers

We are said to be 'anointed by the Spirit' (2 Cor. 1:21). We have an anointing from the Holy One and we all know the truth (1 John 2:20, 27).

Christ Himself was anointed. Indeed 'Messiah' or 'Christ' means 'anointed one'. He is said to be anointed with the oil of joy (Heb. 1:9). Christ has the fullness of the Spirit – from Him we receive our measure of the Spirit. So He is anointed above us, 'that in all things he may have the pre-eminence'.

Isaiah 11:2-3 spells it out: 'The Spirit of the LORD will rest on him – the Spirit of wisdom and of understanding, the Spirit of counsel and of power, the Spirit of knowledge and of the fear of the LORD – and he will delight in the fear of the LORD.'

The purpose of the anointing is to teach us. That was the great promise of the Comforter – that He would 'teach us' (John 14:26), that He would 'guide us into all truth' (John 16:13).

There is a threefold teaching by the Spirit:

(a) A teaching of the Spirit of conviction and illumination. The Spirit teaches the world by the preaching of the word, as He is promised to do in John 16:8.

(b) A teaching of the Spirit of regeneration: opening blind spiritual eyes, giving a new understanding, shining into our hearts to give us a knowledge of the glory of God in the face of Jesus Christ, enabling us to receive spiritual things (1 Cor. 2:13), giving a saving knowledge of the gospel.

(c) A teaching by the Spirit of encouragement: making sweet, useful and joyful to the soul the discoveries that are made of the mind and will of God in the light of the Spirit of sanctification. Here the oil of the Spirit is called the 'oil of joy', bringing joy and gladness with it, and the name of Christ is thus discovered to be sweet perfume poured out. We see in daily experience that very many have little taste and relish in their souls of those truths which they savingly know and believe, but when they are taught by this power, then how sweet is everything we know of God! This is what John means when he writes about this anointing (1 John 2:20) – the Spirit teaching us deeply the love of God in Christ, the smile of His face, which, says David, puts gladness into our hearts (Ps. 4:6-7).

We have these blessings then, by the Spirit – He teaches us the love of God in Christ; He makes every gospel truth taste like finest wine, and a feast of rich food for our souls; He gives us joy and gladness of heart with all that we know of God, which is the great protection for the soul to keep it close to the truth. It is the means whereby we are protected from temptation. Indeed, to know any truth in its real power, sweetness, and joy is the great security for the retention of it. A person will easily change truth for error, when he finds no more sweetness in the one over the other, but when truth is sweet error loses its attraction.

All the privileges we enjoy, all the dignity we have as Christians, our whole dedication to God, our spiritual royalty, all our approach to God in worship, our separation from the ways of the world, the freedom we enjoy – all come to us from this source, the anointing by the Holy Spirit. When we find that any of the good truths of the gospel come home to our hearts with life, vitality and power, giving us gladness of heart, transforming us into the image of Christ – then we know that the Holy Spirit is at His work, pouring His 'oil' into our lives.

8. Adoption

We also have adoption by the Spirit. He is called the 'Spirit of adoption' – that is, the one who makes our adoption real in God's family through Jesus Christ, and the One who reassures us that it is so, that we are God's children (Gal. 4:6).

9. Prayer

He is also called the 'Spirit of prayer' – He enables Christians to pray. We are therefore to 'pray in the Holy Spirit' (Jude 20; and compare Rom. 8:15, 26 and Gal. 4:6).Our prayers may be considered in two ways:

(a) As a duty which God requires of us. The Spirit helps us perform all our duties, by strengthening our souls.

(b) As a way of maintaining fellowship with God – where we receive fresh experience of our Father's love. The soul is never more aware of the love of God than when it is taken by the Spirit into intimate fellowship with Him through prayer. And in this respect it is a work of the Spirit of consolation, the Comforter.

This then is the work of the Holy Spirit: bringing the promises of Christ to our memory, glorifying Christ in our hearts, pouring out the love of God into our hearts, making us aware of our spiritual position and condition, sealing us for the day of full redemption (as the guarantee of the good things to come), confirming our adoption as sons of God, and being present with us in prayer.

And this means that the wisdom of faith is to find out and to meet with the Comforter in all these things, not to lose their sweetness by being ignorant of their source, nor failing to give Him the praise for them.

13.
The effects of the Holy Spirit
in the heart of a believer

1. Encouragement is a consequence of the Holy Spirit in the heart of a believer

'The church … was strengthened; and encouraged by the Holy Spirit, it grew in numbers, living in the fear of the Lord' (Acts 9:31). He is the Comforter and He gives comfort or encouragement. This is the first consequence of His work. Whenever there is mention made of comfort or encouragement given to believers in the Bible (as there often is), it is always a consequence of the work of the Holy Spirit. Comfort is the composure and contentment of the soul in the middle of trouble, by the consideration or presence of some good which outweighs the evil, trouble or perplexity with which it has to wrestle. Wherever there is comfort and consolation, there must also be trouble and perplexity; so the apostle writes in 2 Corinthians 1:5-6, 'For just as the sufferings of Christ flow over into our lives, so also through Christ our comfort overflows'. All the promises of Old and New Testament are given as relief for our suffering.

The effects or acts of the Holy Spirit are the only source of our comfort and encouragement. There is no comfort except from Him, and there is no trouble that we may not have His comfort in.

For a person to have comfort in any condition, nothing is required but the presence of something good, making the evil or suffering being experienced insignificant. Whatever happens to the child of God, whatever evils experienced, even all those mentioned in Romans 8:35-39 – so long as there is also the comfort of the Holy Spirit, that believer's comfort will overflow. Suppose that the heart is full of the sense of the love of God—a clear witness of the Spirit within as a child of God, accepted by God, sealed and marked by God for Himself, that there is an inheritance of all the promises of God, and so on – it is impossible that such a person shall not win through all his troubles.

2. What kind of encouragement does the Comforter provide?

(a) *Lasting* encouragement: The Apostle Paul refers to it in 2 Thessalonians 2:16 as 'eternal encouragement'. It will not disappear. We have this from the Holy Spirit – eternal love, eternal redemption and an eternal inheritance.

(b) *Strong* encouragement: Hebrews 6:18, 'greatly encouraged'. Our opposition may be strong, but so is our encouragement. It is plentiful and it is invincible, unquenchable. It will overcome all opposition, it strengthens the heart, it is from Him who is strong.

(c) *Precious* encouragement: it is so precious that the apostle Paul makes it the great motive for obedience. 'If you have any encouragement from being united with Christ, if any comfort from his love, if any fellowship with the Spirit…' (Phil. 2:1).

3. Peace is another consequence of the Spirit

'May the God of hope fill you with all joy and peace as you trust in him, so that you may overflow with hope by the power of the Holy Spirit' (Rom. 15:13).

It is the same in Christ's words in John 15. 'I will give you the Comforter' – and what then? What will He give them? – Peace '… my peace I give to you'. Christ does not otherwise leave His peace with them or give His peace to them except with the gift of the Comforter. The peace of Christ consists in the soul's sense of its acceptance with God in friendship. In this sense, Christ is 'our peace' (Eph. 2:14), by destroying the hostility between God and us and abolishing the charge written against us. 'Justified by faith we have peace with God' (Rom. 5:1). The basis of this peace is the persuasion that we have been accepted by God, and wrapped up with it there is deliverance from eternal wrath, curse, condemnation – all having a sweet effect on the soul and conscience.

This is, like the others, an effect of the Holy Spirit. Suppose someone is chosen by the eternal love of the Father, redeemed by the blood of the Son, and justified freely by the grace of God, so that he has a right to all the promises of the gospel. That person still cannot be brought to settled peace by any consideration of the promises or the love of God or the grace of Christ, until it is produced in him as a fruit and result of the work of the Holy Spirit in him. 'Peace' is a fruit of the Spirit (Gal. 5:22). 'The mind controlled by the Spirit is life and peace' (Rom. 8:6). All we have is from Him and by Him.

4. Joy is a further consequence of the Spirit
The Spirit is called the 'oil of joy' in Hebrews 1:9. His anointing brings gladness with it. The Apostle Paul says, 'The kingdom of God is a matter righteousness, peace and joy in the Holy Spirit' (Rom. 14:17), and 'you welcomed the message with the joy given by the Holy Spirit' (1 Thess. 1:6).

The Apostle Peter refers to the 'inexpressible and glorious joy' experienced by believers (1 Pet. 1:8). To give joy to the hearts of believers is eminently the work of the Comforter.

There are two ways the Holy Spirit produces joy in the hearts of believers.

(a) Directly – by Himself. He immediately works in the human soul to give a happy, spiritual frame of mind – not something that arises as a result of our reflection on the love of God – it is prior to that and gives rise to that. When He pours out the love of God in our hearts, and so fills them in a direct way (as He caused John the Baptist to leap for joy in the womb at the approach of the mother of Jesus) – then the soul raises itself to consider the love of God, from where joy begins to flow.

(b) Indirectly – through His other activities. By His other activities towards us, He gives a sense of the love of God: by the assurance He gives us of the love of God, the life, power, security, the guarantee of eternal well-being – all these indirectly form a foundation of joy and gladness. Not that we are able simply by our own rational consideration to affect our hearts with joy and gladness, that is still the work of the Holy Spirit alone, who gives us joy both though an appreciation of these things and in a direct way. This process of producing joy in the heart we have referred to in Psalm 23:5-6 'you anoint my head with oil'. Then there is the conclusion, 'Surely goodness and love will follow me'. See also Isaiah, chapter 35, throughout the chapter.

5. Hope is also an effect of the work of the Holy Spirit in us (Rom. 15:13)

These then are the general consequences of the Holy Spirit living in the Christian believer, and we might also consider their offshoots in assurance, boldness, confidence, expectation and so on.

14.
Getting the right balance

We should be careful to get the right balance when it comes to an appreciation of the Holy Spirit. Some virtually ignore Him in their version of 'Christianity', others seem to lack discernment as to what is His work and what is not.

We need to say first of all that the Holy Spirit is essential. The work of Christ achieves nothing without the work of the Spirit following it. This is the state of things – that in our worship of God, our obedience to God, our encouragement, our sanctification and Christian activity, the Spirit is the fundamental source, the life, the soul of it all.

Yet there are false spirits in the world, counterfeits of the real thing. And we must test the spirits to make sure they are from God, the authentic work of the Holy Spirit and not some other spirit, the spirit of the world. We need to recognise false spirits from the true Holy Spirit. Satan has the ability to transform himself into an angel of light and pretend to be what he is not, namely, the Holy Spirit.

We must examine the differences in the effects of the Holy Spirit and the effects of the spirit of the world.

The first general consequence of the work of the Holy Spirit is this: that He should remind us of Christ's teaching, for our guidance and encouragement. This was to be the work of the Holy Spirit towards the apostles, who were to be the writers of the Scriptures. The authentic work of the Holy Spirit is to remind us of Christ's words, the words of God in Scripture. The things that Christ has spoken and done are written that you might believe, and believing, have life in His name (John 20:31) – they are written in the Bible.

But the work of the spirit of the world is altogether different: it pretends that there are new revelations from God, leading men and women away from the Bible, where the whole work of God and all the promises of Christ are recorded.

The work of the Spirit promised by Christ is to glorify Christ: 'He will bring glory to me by taking from what is mine and making it known to you' (John 16:14). However, the work of the spirit of the world is to glorify itself, to decry Christ. This is precisely how we identify the false spirit – it does not emphasise Christ but the self.

Furthermore, the Holy Spirit pours the love of God into our hearts, and so fills us with joy, peace and hope; He calms and refreshes the hearts of those in whom He lives; He gives us freedom, rest, confidence, and the assurance of children. However, the spirit of the world is entirely different. It is a spirit of slavery. It makes people fearful, unwilling to follow Christ. It is in direct opposition to the Spirit who lives in believers.

To give one further example of the difference between the work of the Holy Spirit and the work of the spirit of the world: the Holy Spirit given to believers is a Spirit of prayer and petition, but the spirit of the world would have us believe that this is a poor way to have communion with God and so despises prayer.

In summary, it would be an easy task to show how the spirit of the world opposes every aspect of the Holy Spirit's work. This is the work of Satan himself, who not only opposes the Spirit of Christ, but attempts to imitate Him in false ways.

15.
The value of the encouragement of the Holy Spirit

1. There are just three things in the whole course of our Christian life and in each of these the strength of the Holy Spirit is essential:

(a) In our suffering

Suffering is an integral part of our Christian life and experience for now (Heb. 12:5, 6). In all our sufferings we need the encouragement and strengthening of the Holy Spirit.

We can fall into two extremes (both of which are mentioned in Heb. 12:5):

  (a) We can fail to see God's discipline in it. We can fail to use the suffering to lead us to the strength of the Holy Spirit.

  (b) We can become discouraged and sink under it. This attitude is reproved in Hebrews 12:12. The first despises the assistance of the Holy Spirit through pride of heart; the second refuses it through dejection of spirit, and sinks under the weight of these troubles.

There is no right management of our souls when in trouble so that God gets the glory from it, and we get spiritual benefit or improvement from it, *except by the strength of the Holy Spirit.* All that our Saviour promises His disciples when He tells them of the great troubles they are to undergo is, 'I will send you the Spirit, the Comforter; he will give you peace in me, when in the world you will have trouble'. And so it was in the life of the apostle Paul (2 Cor. 1:4-6) and under the greatest pressure – the Spirit can carry the soul to the greatest joy, peace, rest, and contentment. The same apostle wrote (Rom. 5:1-5), 'We rejoice in suffering' – a remarkable expression. He had said before, 'We rejoice in the hope of the glory of God' (v. 2). Yes, but what if *many* troubles come our way? 'Why', he says, 'even in them you can also rejoice.' But how is it that our spirits are so lifted up that we can actually rejoice? He tells us in verse 5 – it is from the Holy Spirit who pours out the love of God into our hearts. And for this reason believers are said to welcome the word in great affliction, with joy given by the Holy Spirit (1 Thess. 1:6) and to joyfully accept the confiscation of their property (Heb. 10:34). This is what we aim at – that there is no handling of any trouble, except with the help of the Holy Spirit. Learn then, to value your troubles and the Holy Spirit who alone can make them useful to you.

(b) In our sin

Sin is the second burden of our lives, and by far the greatest. Here the strength of the Holy Spirit is particularly suited.

Our great and only refuge from the guilt of sin is the Lord Jesus Christ; when we run to Him, the Spirit applies His encouragement to us. A sense of sin fills the human heart with turmoil; it is the Holy Spirit who gives us peace of mind through Christ. Satan and the law accuse us, as objects of God's hatred; but the Spirit bears witness with our spirits that we are children of God.

(c) In obedience

In the whole of our obedience His encouragements are necessary, that we may continue our Christian lives cheerfully, willingly, and patiently to the end. In short, in all the concerns of this life, and all our anticipation of the next, we stand in need of the strength of the Holy Spirit.

Without this strength, we shall either despise our troubles or sink under them, and God will be forgotten as to His purpose in them. Without it, sin will either harden us or cast us down so that we fail to use the remedies God provides. Without it, duties will either puff us up with pride, or leave us without that sweetness which is in new obedience. Without it, prosperity will make us materialistic, looking for our contentment in these things, and utterly weaken us for the trials of adversity. Without it, the failures of the church will overwhelm us, and the success of the church will not concern us. Without it, we shall have concern for no spiritual work, peace in no condition, strength for no duty, success in no trial, joy in no state – no comfort in life, no light in death.

Now, our troubles, our sins and our obedience are the great businesses of life. What we are in relation to God consists in these things. Through all these there runs a line of encouragement from the Holy Spirit, which gives us a joyful outcome throughout. How sad is the condition of bankrupt souls destitute of His encouragement! What problems they must encounter with only their own strength! And whether they are conquered, or *seem* to conquer, they have nothing to experience but the misery of their trials!

2. But now we must consider a further matter: what does the Holy Spirit comfort and encourage us with? The answer to

that is this: He comforts us with the love of the Father and the grace of the Son.

(a) He communicates to us and makes us familiar with the love of the Father. Having informed His disciples of the coming of the Comforter into their lives, the Lord Jesus concludes with these words: 'The Father himself loves you' (John 16:27). This is why the Comforter is given to us – to assure us that God is the Father and that He loves us. By persuading us of the eternal and unchangeable love of the Father, the Holy Spirit fills us with comfort. A sense of this love is able not only to comfort us, but in every condition to make us rejoice with an inexpressible and glorious joy. 'The world may hate me', the Christian who has the Holy Spirit may say, 'but my Father loves me. Men despise me as a hypocrite, but my Father loves me as a child. I am poor in this world, but I have a rich inheritance in the love of my Father. I mourn secretly over the sin and its power in my life, but the Father sees me and is full of compassion. With a sense of His kindness, which is better than life, I rejoice in trouble, glory in suffering, overcome like a conqueror'. There is no comparison with the joy and comfort we receive from the Spirit who comes to us with the love of the Father.

(b) He communicates to us, and makes us familiar with, the grace of Christ – all the effects of His redemption, all the beauty of His person. The grace of Christ refers to both the grace of His person and to the grace of His work. By both of these the Holy Spirit supplies His comfort to us (John 16:14). He glorifies Christ by revealing His excellencies and desirableness to believers and then He shows them the character of Christ – His love, grace, all the results of His death, suffering, resurrection, and mediation: and with these He supports their hearts and souls.

(c) We must also consider the Holy Spirit's own great love and condescension. For He willingly comes from the Father to be our Comforter. He knew what we were like, how we would grieve Him, provoke Him, quench His power, defile His residence in our hearts – and yet still He came to be our Comforter. Failure to give real consideration to the great love of the Holy Spirit will weaken our obedience. Let us consider the great value we should put on all His activity in our lives!

This is how the Bible leads us to a right appreciation of our redemption in Jesus Christ. It tells us that He did it freely, that He did it out of love. 'This is how we know what love is: Jesus Christ laid down his life for us' (1 John 3:16); '[he] loved me and gave himself for me' (Gal. 2:20); 'to him who loves us and has freed us from our sins by his blood' (Rev. 1:5). The Bible adds to this our state and condition – sinners, enemies, dead, alienated – then He loved us, and died for us, and washed us in His blood. May we not also have an appreciation of the Spirit's comfort in our lives?

Let us by faith consider this love of the Holy Spirit. It is the source of all the fellowship we have with Him in this life.

16.
Life in the Holy Spirit

There are three general ways of life lived in fellowship with the Holy Spirit – all expressed negatively in the Bible, but all including positive responsibilities:

1. not to grieve Him,

2. not to quench His activity,

3. not to resist Him.

There are three things to consider in relation to the Holy Spirit himself:

1. His person, living in us,

2. His activity of grace,

3. His working in and through the word of God and the sacraments.

Corresponding to these three are three cautions previously noted:

1. not to grieve Him, in relation to His person living in us,

2. not to quench Him, in relation to His activity,

3. not to resist Him, in relation to the commands of Christ.

1. The first caution concerns the 'person' of the Holy Spirit, who lives within us. It is given in Ephesians 4:30: 'Do not grieve the Holy Spirit of God'. For example, in Isaiah 63:10 there is a complaint about those who vexed or grieved the Spirit of God.

   The Holy Spirit behaves towards us as One who is loving, tender, concerned for our good and doing good; and therefore when we sin He is grieved, just as a good friend with a kind and loving nature is apt to be offended by us. And this is what we are to appreciate as the foundation of His grief – the love, kindness and tenderness of the Holy Spirit towards us. 'Do not grieve him'.

   Positively, we must pursue holiness because of the love, kindness and tenderness of the Holy Spirit towards us. This is the foundation of all our fellowship with Him. We need to consider the love, kindness and tenderness of the Holy Spirit towards us. We should reflect on all the results and acts of His love toward us. If we then understand that the Holy Spirit is so concerned about all our ways that we seek to abstain from sin and to live in holiness – this is what it means to have fellowship with Him. Make it your continual motive and reason for close walking with God in all holiness that the Holy Spirit is delighted with our obedience and grieved with our sin. This is our first general way to have fellowship with Him.

   Let us concentrate a little further on this. We lose both the power and pleasure of our obedience if we do not think about this general means of fellowship. We see on what account the Holy Spirit undertakes to be our Comforter, by what ways and means He performs that service towards us, and so realise what an unworthy thing it is to grieve Him who comes to us for the purpose of giving us encouragement! Let us say to our souls, 'The Holy Spirit, in His infinite love and kindness towards me, has condescended to be my Comforter; He does it willingly, freely, powerfully. What I have received from Him! In all the many difficulties of my life, how He has refreshed my soul! Can I live one day without His encouragements? And will I ignore the things that concern Him? Will I grieve Him by negligence, sin and foolishness? Will not His love constrain me to live before Him in a way that pleases Him?, So shall we have fellowship with Him.

2. The second caution appears in 1 Thessalonians 5:19, 'Quench not the Spirit' (AV). There are various understandings of these words. The Holy Spirit was typified in the Old Testament by the fire that was always kept alive on the altar. Fire is 'opposed' by quenching it, as with wet wood. The Holy Spirit is at work in us, working for our growth in grace. Do not hinder Him, do not quench Him. This then is the second general rule for our fellowship with the Holy Spirit. It concerns His gracious operations in us and by us.

Thus we have fellowship with the Holy Spirit, when we can consider Him by faith as the immediate source of all the help we have by grace, the source of all good intentions and actions, of all our efforts against sin. When we consider all these actions of the Holy Spirit for our strengthening, and on that account are careful and alert to foster them, and as we appreciate that they come from Him who is so loving, and kind, and tender to us, then we will have real fellowship with Him.

3. The third caution concerns the Holy Spirit and His work, as the giver of the word of God. Stephen warned the Jews that they 'resisted the Holy Spirit' (Acts 7:51). How? As their forefathers did. How did their forefathers resist the Holy Spirit? They persecuted the prophets and killed them (v. 52). Their opposition to the prophets in the preaching of the gospel, or their prediction of the coming of the Messiah, was their resisting of the Holy Spirit. The Holy Spirit is said to be resisted where there is contempt of preaching because the gift of preaching the gospel is from Him. So, when Christ promised the Spirit to His disciples, to be with them for the conviction of the world, He tells them He will give them ability and words to speak which their enemies will not be able to refute or resist (Luke 21:15). Thus, it is said of Stephen that his enemies 'could not stand up against his wisdom or the Spirit by whom he spoke' (Acts 6:10).

And this includes the third general rule of our communion with the Holy Spirit – we are to be subject to the word of God. For this reason we are to give our obedience to the word – because the Holy Spirit gave it. When this consideration causes us to humble ourselves before the word, then (again) we have fellowship with the Holy Spirit.

17.
Directions for fellowship with the Holy Spirit

Before giving particular directions, I must give some cautions concerning the worship of the Holy Spirit.

1. God's divine nature is the reason and cause of all worship, so it is impossible to worship any one person, and not worship the whole Trinity. The proper and particular object of worship and prayer is the 'essence' of God, in its infinite excellence, dignity, majesty, and sovereignty. This is common to all three persons, and is specific to each of them, as God blessed for ever. Therefore in each act of adoration and worship, all the persons are adored and worshipped. Creatures must worship their Creator.

2. When we begin our prayers to God the Father and end them in the name of Jesus Christ, we worship the Son at the beginning no less than we worship the Father, since in worshipping the Father we worship Father, Son and Holy Spirit. And in prayer to God the Father, we pray to the Son and Spirit too, because we appeal to God as Father and the Son and Spirit are also God.

3. Ephesians 2:18 spells it out clearly for us. Our access in our worship is 'to the Father'; 'through Christ', His

mediation; and 'by the Spirit', His assistance. There is a distinction of persons, in their operations, but no distinction at all as objects of our worship. For the Son and the Holy Spirit are no less worshipped in our access to God than the Father Himself. So that this is what we say concerning the whole matter: that when any work of the Holy Spirit (or any other person) draws us to worship Him, He is not then worshipped exclusively (of Father and Son), but the whole trinitarian God is worshipped.

4. Having set out these qualifications, I now say that we *are* distinctly to worship the Holy Spirit. As it is in the case of faith in relation to the Father and the Son, 'Trust in God, trust also in me' (John 14:1) – this extends no less to the Holy Spirit. We worship Jesus not only because He is our mediator but because He is God. In the same way we worship the Holy Spirit not only because He is our Comforter but because He is God.

This is the summary of the first point: the grace, activity, love, effect of the Holy Spirit, as our Comforter, ought to stir us up and cause us to love, worship, believe in, and pray to Him – though all this, being directed to Him as God, is no less directed to the Father and Son than to the Holy Spirit.

Let us have a faith that recognises His kindness in all things. Frequently, He acts as a Comforter towards us, and we are not comforted – we take no notice of what He is doing. Then He is grieved. Of all those who do receive His encouragement, how few are there who consider Him as the Comforter and rejoice in Him as they ought! With every encouragement that the believer receives, this should be the resolve: 'This is from the Holy Spirit; He is the Comforter, the God of all comfort; I know there is no joy, peace, hope, nor comfort, except what He produces and gives; and that He might give me this strength, He has willingly condescended to this role of a Comforter. His love was in it. What price I will set upon His love! How I will value the mercy I have received!'

This is applicable to every particular influence of the Holy Spirit towards us, and in this we have fellowship with Him. Does He pour out the love of God in our hearts? Does He witness with our spirits that we are children of God? The soul considers His presence, thinks about His love, His condescension, goodness and kindness; is filled with reverence of Him, and takes care not to grieve Him, but makes every effort to preserve His temple (ourselves) pure and holy.

Again, our intimacy with Him gives rise to praise within us, and thanks, honour, glory to Him, for the mercies we receive from Him – which are many. We praise the Son for our redemption: 'To him who loves us and has freed us from our sins by his blood … to him be glory and power for ever and ever!' (Rev. 1:5-6). Are not the same praises due to Him by whom Christ's work of redemption is applied to us, namely the Holy Spirit? When we feel our hearts warmed with joy, supported by peace, established in obedience, let us give to Him the praise that He deserves, and rejoice in Him.

And this glorifying of the Holy Spirit in praise is no small part of our fellowship with Him. There is no duty that leaves a more heavenly taste in the soul than this.

Also, in our prayers to Him to carry on the work of sanctification which He has begun in our lives, lies our fellowship with Him. We must ask for Him from the Father in the name of Jesus Christ. This is to be the daily work of believers. Believers know that in this promise of the Holy Spirit lies all their grace, peace, mercy, joy and hope. For these things are communicated to them by the promised Spirit, and by Him alone.

Let us ask the Father for the Holy Spirit just as children ask their parents for their daily bread. And as we receive the Holy Spirit, so we have communication with the love of the Father and the grace of the Son. Every request for the Holy Spirit includes our drawing near to the love of the Father and the grace of the Son. O the riches of the grace of God!

Humbling ourselves for our offences against Him is another aspect of our communication with Him. We should mourn that we have grieved Him personally, that we have quenched the actions of His grace, or resisted His word. Let our souls be humbled before Him because of these things.

5. I will close this discussion with consideration of the sad condition of those who have no interest in the promise of the Spirit, nor any experience of His grace.

(a) They have no real *comfort*. If they are under pressure or in trouble, they must bear their own burden – and it is clear that they are too weak to bear it alone. Some people may have naturally strong spirits and great determination to wrestle with their problems, but then this is only in their natural strength:

(i) For the most part this is just external show. It is one with respect to others, that they may not appear low-spirited or dejected. In reality they are full of anxiety. It is a groundless resolution that supports them, and they are easily upset.

(ii) What is their determination and perseverance like? Just like a flea struggling under the weight of a mountain, a contending with God who has entangled them. God does not trouble men without the

Spirit in order to exercise their patience, but to disturb their peace and security. All their arming themselves with patience and resolution is nothing more than an attempt to secure their lives against God.

(iii) If they do pretend to have some help from God – as they often do, especially when they are driven from other securities – all their relief is just like the dreaming of a hungry man, who imagines that he is eating and drinking and being refreshed, but when he awakes, he finds that he is still empty and disappointed. So all the relief they pretend to receive from God is no more than a dream. When they are spiritually awakened, on the Last Day, and see everything clearly, they will find that God was always their enemy, not their friend and support as they foolishly imagined.

Is it any better with them in their prosperity? Their wealth, indeed, is often considerable, and is marvellously described in the Bible, concerning their lives and often peaceful deaths. But do they have any *true* consolation all their days? They eat, drink, sleep and make merry, and perhaps store up possessions for themselves, but how little do these things make them different from animals! So that both adversity and prosperity destroy them, and whether they are laughing or crying, they are still dying.

(b) They have no real *peace* – no peace with God and no peace in their own souls. Real and solid peace is a consequence of the Holy Spirit in the heart, and those who do not have Him do not have peace. They may pretend there is peace when there is no peace (Jer. 6:14). The principles of their peace (which are easy to prove) are ignorance, deception of conscience, self-righteousness, and empty hope. And what good will these principles do them on the day of judgement?

(c) They have no real *joy and hope*. There are those who say they are interested in the gospel of Christ, but have despised the Spirit of Christ. Let them think about this: the Bible says that unless the Spirit of Christ is in us, we do not belong to Christ. If the Holy Spirit does not live in you, if He is not your Comforter, then neither is God your Father, nor the Son your Advocate, nor do you have any share in the gospel. May God awaken such people to their own condition before it is too late and they are lost for ever!

The Experience That Counts

Jonathan Edwards

What does it mean to be a Christian? Is Christianity a matter of the intellect alone? What about desires, feelings,

and experiences? What is conversion? These questions are not new, Jonathan Edwards, the great American theologian tackled these, and many other, against the background of the First Great Awakening.

These questions, and the answers Edwards gives to them, are profoundly relevant to us today.

Find 'a guide for the perplexed' – a voice of clear Biblical and spiritual sanity to lead us safely through the maze of contemporary confusion in this crucial area.

Jonathan Edwards (1703-1758) was foremost leader of the Great Awakening in North America in the 18th Century.

ISBN 978-1-78191-719-0

Christian Freedom

SAMUEL BOLTON

Christian Freedom provides an accessible entry into Samuel Bolton's original work, *The True Bounds of Christian Freedom*, first published in 1645. This book is not simply an academic discussion of the issues; Samuel Bolton constantly reminds his readers of the gospel, and the great transformation that has happened to a person who has trusted in Jesus Christ. Bolton shows us clearly that real Christian obedience comes from a changed heart, and is motivated by love for God. He deals with the practical question of what happens when Christians fall into sin, and encourages us to rely on what. Christ has done for us, rather than on our performance.

Samuel Bolton (1606-1654) was an English clergyman and scholar, a member of the Westminster Assembly and Master of Christ's College, Cambridge.

ISBN 978-1-78191-721-3

The Glory of Christ

John Owen

To see the glory of Christ is one of the greatest privileges that a Christian can enjoy. Anyone who does not see his

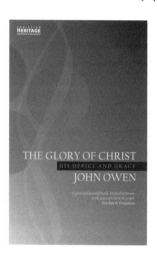

glory in this world, will not see his glory in heaven, and no one should look for anything in heaven that he has not experienced in this life. Read this book, and may God by his Word and Spirit give you such a sense of his uncreated glory, blazing forth in Christ, that you will be satisfied and filled with joy. This is the orginal text with a new layout and is fully subtitled which makes it more accessible to a new generation of readers.

I'm here today, absolutely certain that the subject we ought to think about together is the glory of Christ. And John Owen's book on the Glory of Christ is the classic writing on that subject. ...I commend that book to you very warmly and anything that I've learned of the Glory of Christ you will find elaborated considerably there.

Eric Alexander
Conference speaker and formerly minister St George's Tron,
Glasgow for 20 years

ISBN 978-1-85792-474-9

Communion with God

John Owen

In 1657, John Owen produced one of his finest devotional treatrises: probably originating from the substance of a series of sermons.

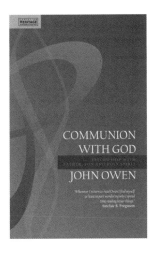

This was a controversial work in ecclesiastical circles of the 17th century. Twenty years after its publication, the rational ecclesiastical elite were scoffing at it's contents. Owen strongly defended the ideas within this book, and history has shown him to be right! It is a classic of Christian devotional thought that still influences the church today. This is the orginal text with a new layout and is fully subtitled which makes it more accessible to a new generation of readers.

Owen was by common consent the weightiest Puritan theologian, and many would bracket him with Jonathan Edwards as one of the greatest Reformed theologians of all time.

J. I. Packer

Well known Author & Board of Governors' Professor of Theology, Regent College, Vancouver, Canada

ISBN 978-1-84550-209-6

Christian Focus Publications

Our mission statement –

STAYING FAITHFUL

In dependence upon God we seek to impact the world through literature faithful to His infallible Word, the Bible. Our aim is to ensure that the Lord Jesus Christ is presented as the only hope to obtain forgiveness of sin, live a useful life and look forward to heaven with Him.

Our books are published in four imprints:

CHRISTIAN
FOCUS

Popular works including biographies, commentaries, basic doctrine and Christian living.

CHRISTIAN
HERITAGE

Books representing some of the best material from the rich heritage of the church.

MENTOR

Books written at a level suitable for Bible College and seminary students, pastors, and other serious readers. The imprint includes commentaries, doctrinal studies, examination of current issues and church history.

CF4•K

Children's books for quality Bible teaching and for all age groups: Sunday school curriculum, puzzle and activity books; personal and family devotional titles, biographies and inspirational stories – because you are never too young to know Jesus!

Christian Focus Publications Ltd,
Geanies House, Fearn, Ross-shire,
IV20 1TW, Scotland, United Kingdom.
www.christianfocus.com